D0408488

No American, thinking back over our nation's history, can doubt the value of the religious liberty we have won. But today Christians have come to take religious freedom somewhat for granted as a natural law of social progress. In this brilliant and fascinating book, however, Cecil Northcott shows that religious freedom is far from universal, that in many countries it is an aim still to be achieved.

He writes of the challenge of Islam and the lack of religious liberty in Egypt as well as of conditions in Soviet Russia. There is a particularly fair and interesting chapter on the influence of the Catholic Church in Latin American countries. Another chapter deals with the attitude toward missions of various governments throughout the world. The book closes with a plea for tolerance and for respect for the sanctity of the individual.

Religious liberty is undoubtedly threatened in many parts of the modern world. It is important that the situation should be squarely faced and clearly understood.

RELIGIOUS
LIBERTY

RELIGIOUS LIBERTY

BY

CECIL NORTHCOTT

NEW YORK
THE MACMILLAN COMPANY
1949

Copyright, 1948 by
THE MACMILLAN COMPANY

First Printing

CONTENTS

PREFACE

THIS modest contribution to a large and important subject is offered with some trepidation as I am not expertly versed in the theory of religious liberty, nor have I had the experience of living in those lands where full religious liberty is not enjoyed, but I owe much to discussions and conversations with those who live in such countries. In addition I have read as widely as possible recognizing the relevance of the subject in the modern world, and I hope the facts and information in the book will be found practically useful.

The Joint Committee on Religious Liberty, set up in 1946 by the British Council of Churches and the Conference of British Missionary Societies under the chairmanship of Sir Ernest Barker, were good enough to be interested in the book, and some of its members gave me valuable help and advice. The committee have no sort of responsibility for the book, which commits no one—except myself—to its standpoint or opinions.

I am particularly indebted to Dr. Searle Bates' encyclopedic *Religious Liberty: An Inquiry* (International Missionary Council 1945), to the Joint Committee's statement *Human Rights and Religious Freedom* (1947), and to the Editor of *Religion in Life*, New York, Abingdon-Cokesbury Press, for permission to include in Chapter III material which I have contributed to that journal. I have to thank Miss Olga Pilpel, Ph.D., for her competent help with the manuscript.

C.N.

I

WHAT IS RELIGIOUS LIBERTY?

"RELIGIOUS liberty? " queried a friend to whom I mentioned the writing of this book, " haven't we got it? What about nonconformity, freedom of worship, toleration and all that? Surely that battle, at any rate, has been fought and won? " In one sense he was right so far as Britain is concerned.

It is a hundred and twenty years since the Test and Corporation Acts passed into the limbo of old unhappy things of English religious and civil controversy, and no one would now seriously question the right of any group in Britain to freedom of worship, teaching and propaganda. We no longer compel Englishmen when they worship to attend a parish church for a service according to the Anglican prayer book, neither do we clamp civil disabilities on to those who are not members of the Established church. You may, since April 13, 1829, be a Roman Catholic and also aspire to any public office save that of High Commissioner to the General Assembly of the Church of Scotland. You may also, since 1854, obtain a bachelor's degree at Oxford without membership of the Church of England—a reform which wrung Dr. Pusey's heart in the cry, " Oxford is lost to the Church of England. The dam is broken. How soon it will be carried away God only knows." You may, since 1880, be buried in your parish churchyard by a dissenting minister with " a Christian and orderly service ", unobstructed by the rector's private army furnished with pitchforks. Neither do we, as in the days of Presbyterian and Independent ecclesiastical domination, break up Anglican services, attempt to destroy the organ in St. Paul's and order (as in 1643) the " utter demolishing and removing of all monuments of idolatry and superstition out of all churches and chapels in England and Wales ". When it comes to assessing praise and blame in the history of religious freedom there are unwelcome prizes for everyone! How vituperatively Englishmen debated religious truth and error in the formative years of the seventeenth century when by pamphlet and by parliament, by cracked heads and civil war, these islands fashioned a policy of religious toleration —an experience which prompted a 1659 rhymster:

> *Religion's made a tennis-ball*
> *For every fool to play withall,*
> *Both which we have so many,*
> *That we disputed have so long*
> *'Bout which is right, and which is wrong,*
> *Till we have hardly any.*[1]

There were never lacking, however, wise and charitable men like the Puritan Richard Baxter who saw that a religious settlement in England meant that men who differed must learn to live together. " I beseech you ", he wrote, " to give others leave to live in the same house with you . . . nothing so much hindereth the reception of the truth, as urging it on men with too harsh importunity, and falling too heavily on their errors. For hereby you engage their honour in the business, and they defend their errors as themselves, and stir up all their wit and ability to oppose you."[2]

If the growth of religious toleration in England was often a tedious and inglorious procedure, it was also, in character and methods, a peculiarly English achievement—with no excessive theorizing about religious liberty, but much determination to have it, even though it meant for some ostracism, persecution and eventual emigration across the seas.

---

[1] Quoted W. K. Jordan, *The Development of Religious Toleration in England*, Vol. IV, p. 363.
[2] Richard Baxter, *Reliquiae Baxterianae*, I, 125-6.

This country has learned that the price of any liberty is always practical vigilance—a lesson to be well heeded in the modern world.

On the same day as my friend declared the battle won a member of parliament raised in the House of Commons the question of entry into this country of members of a religious fellowship—the Oxford Group. Mr. Chuter Ede, the Home Secretary, in reply said, "I am not prepared to apply religious or political tests to people who desire to come into this country unless it can be established that they desire to come here to carry on subversive propaganda. The common sense of the British democracy is such that, in the long run, they will winnow the chaff from the wheat. I wish that the ancient record of this country as a place of free speech, where the flow of ideas from all parts of the world is welcomed, might be maintained. I desire to impose no censorship other than that which the law entitles me to impose against subversive propaganda, on any particular person who desires to come to this country to meet people of his own persuasion."[1]

A government's right to control entry to a country is one thing, but to exercise it on the grounds of religion would be a high infringement of liberty. Whatever may be said about the particular incident and its circumstances, it is a warning that even in a land where religious tolerance is securely enthroned there may be threats to new developments in organized religion.

I

Whatever may be true in Britain, on the continent of Europe, during the last sixteen years, the threats to religious liberty have been violent and prolonged. On September 14, 1930, when the Nazi membership in the Reichstag jumped

[1] *The Times*, July 6, 1946.

from twelve to one hundred and seven, the churches—both Roman Catholic and Protestant—began to realize that they were faced with a challenge to the Christian religion and its freedom in worship, belief and action. Four years later, in May 1934, the Barmen Synod declaration of the Protestant churches said, " We repudiate the false teaching that the Church can and must recognize as a source of its message, in addition to and beside this one Word of God, also other events and powers, figures and truths as Divine revelation." The religious struggle within Germany during the last sixteen years was essentially one to preserve the life and liberty of the Church in face of a state which, in the Bishop of Berlin's words, would " make of the state a church by determining sermons and creed by force ". In Russia, following the disestablishment of the Church at the revolution in 1917, freedom for the " conduct of religious cults " was granted, and the Stalin constitution of November 1936, defining the position of religion in the Soviet Union says, " freedom for the conduct of religious cults and freedom for anti-religious propaganda is recognized for all citizens ". The *rapprochement* of the war period between State and Church has not altered the legal position of religious associations, and active religious propaganda outside the life of the Church is not permitted.

In Italy by the Concordat of 1929 (re-affirmed by the Republic in 1947) the first article recognizes " the Catholic religion as the sole religion of the State ", and although " admitted cults " (including the Salvation Army and the Pentecostalists) are also recognized in practice, their public preaching and any share in school education is made as difficult as possible. In Spain religious liberty, except for Roman Catholics, scarcely exists. In Japan from 1940-1945 State Shintoism (abolished by General MacArthur's decree, 1946) came perilously near demanding pagan acts from the Christian believer as part of his state allegiance, and the "control" of the recognized religions was subtly geared to the purposes of the state. In Mexico and the Latin American countries the main challenge to religious liberty lies in the obstacles planted in the pathway of missionary freedom.

The lands of Islam present perhaps the most formidable examples of the denial of religious liberty as it is known amongst the Western democracies. Islam—the complete "church-state"—still forbids a change of faith away from Islam under dire penalties, with only Iraq, Palestine and the Northern Sudan possessing regular procedures for the recognition of conversion to another religious allegiance. While Christian and Jewish communities are allowed to remain in comparatively undisturbed peace, economic and cultural pressure on non-Islamic groups is formidable. In Egypt, for instance, the ancient Christian Coptic community loses hundreds of members each year to Islam for economic and matrimonial reasons.

This rapid survey of the chief danger points for religious liberty (which will be dealt with in more detail in the Survey chapters) is evidence that we are dealing with an issue of world importance, and one which pertinently affects the liberties of the individual man, the freedom of religious worship and the right of any religious faith to be a propagating faith. For Christianity, and this book has in mind particularly the problem of religious liberty as it affects Christianity, the issues are of crucial importance, especially in Islamic lands where the future of the Christian faith may well be precarious, and in the territories of Eastern nations such as China, India and Indonesia—destined to have a strategic share in shaping the new life of the world. Even in the United States of America, States have been known to protect their religious life by using the secular arm to prevent the doctrine of evolution from being taught!

II

But what exactly is religious liberty? No definition will be entirely satisfactory to everyone. As Dr. Searle Bates remarks in his *Inquiry*,[1] " to some it is an utter individualism; to others the unhindered power of a mighty ecclesiastical system. To some it implies open competition of religious bodies; to others unity protected and undisturbed. To some it means the right to challenge a traditional religion which is the sanction for moral and social standards among a large majority of the members of a nation; to others it is the right to protect a cherished religion against modernism or foreign doctrines or atheism."

Liberty itself is often defined as an absence of compulsion or restraint; but liberty must be more than a mere negative. If there is no opportunity to choose there is no real freedom and no growth in moral responsibility. Lord Acton's definition, " By liberty I mean the assurance that every man shall be protected in doing what he believes his duty against the influence of authority and majorities, custom and opinion "[2] is more inclusive and understanding than J. S. Mill's famous definition, "The only freedom which deserves the name is that of pursuing our own good in our own way; so long as we do not attempt to deprive others of theirs, or impede their efforts to obtain it."[3] But William Penn's definition comes nearer than any of them for our purpose in stating clearly the central factor in any definition of religious liberty—the natural right of conscience:

I ever understood an impartial liberty of conscience to be the natural right of all men, and that he that had a religion without it, his religion was none of his own. For what is not the religion of a man's choice is the religion

[1] Bates, *Religious Liberty: An Inquiry*, p. 302.
[2] Acton, *History of Freedom*, p. 3.
[3] J. S. Mill, *On Liberty*, Chap. I.

of him that imposes it: so that liberty of conscience is the first step to have a religion.[1]

The first element, then, in freedom of religion must be freedom to choose one's religion.

Jacques Maritain has eloquently stated the two-sidedness of this power of choice, " *With respect to God and truth,* one has not the right to choose according to his own whim any path whatsoever, he must choose the true path, in so far as it is in his power to know it. But *with respect to the State, to the temporal community and to the temporal power,* he is free to choose his religious path at his own risk, his freedom of conscience is a natural, inviolable right."[2] It is only when his choices " lead to acts repugnant to natural law and the security of the State that the latter has the right to interfere and apply sanctions against these acts. This does not mean that it has authority in the realm of conscience "[3]—a fact well established in Britain after two wars, in the position of the conscientious objector to armed service.

But choices cannot be made in isolation. Liberty is a social experience in which a man's choice affects others as well as himself. The really free man finds his personality developing in fellowship with others whether on a large scale like a state or church, or in a smaller community such as a family. Religion especially implies a relationship with God and the enjoyment of that relationship in association with other men. It implies a community loyalty and corporate acts of worship in which the individual is involved in the life of a group, that group being related to other groups.

" When I speak of a lover of religious freedom," wrote Mr. Gladstone, " I mean one who, desiring the full enjoy-

[1] William Penn, *England's Present Interest Considered*, quoted Bates, op. cit., p. 297.
[2] Jacques Maritain, *The Rights of Man and Natural Law*, pp. 45-6.
[3] ibid., p. 46.

ment of it for his own communion, is not willing only, but anxious, as he prizes the sacred principle of justice, to accord to all other religious bodies precisely the same measure, and to guard against all secular interference in their concerns, so long as they do not trespass upon the sphere of secular affairs. . . . As with property, so with religious freedom: the rights of each man are the rights of his neighbour; he that defends one is the defender of all; and he that trespasses on one assails all."[1]

Compare this with Lord Acton who, in a similar vein, held that " it is the right of all religious communities to the practice of their own duties, the enjoyment of their own constitution, and the protection of the law, which equally secures to all the possession of their own independence. . . . This freedom is attainable only in communities where rights are sacred and where law is supreme."[2]

Lord Acton (and many other thinkers in this field) believed that religious liberty was best secured in a state where there was a " limited " toleration, as for instance in England where the state itself has some " religious character ", rather than in a state without any definite religious character where, he believed, no genuine ecclesiastical authority could exist and, therefore, no true understanding of all that is meant by religious liberty. This limited " toleration "—often called Jurisdictionalism, i.e. some supervision by the state as in England—is opposed by Separatism, i.e. the complete separation of the two powers ecclesiastical and civil, of which the two most complete examples are in France and in the United States of America.

Both systems have secured in the countries of their adoption large measures of religious liberty—neither of them, however, entirely free from defects. For instance, it can be historically shown that Separatism has hardly been

[1] Gladstone, *Letter on the Functions of Laymen in the Church*, p. 13 (quoted A. R. Vidler, *The Orb and the Cross*, p. 89).
[2] Acton, op. cit., p. 151.

favourable to the liberty of the individual conscience. The single congregation has often been a petty tyrant, and in the early days of the American colonies the system was intolerant of any form of error. But Separatism has undoubtedly been the most favourable towards absolute liberty of worship. The other system, Jurisdictionalism, while less favourable towards liberty of worship, has often been a guarantee of liberty of conscience. It is not our business here to debate the merits of the two systems, but to point out that the idea of religious liberty is really independent of them, and that the practical test of it in any country is whether there is for the individual liberty of conscience, and for churches liberty of worship and witness. It is these liberties which in a country where " rights are sacred and where law is supreme " are secured by law—a fact which renders religious liberty an essentially juridical idea even more than it is a theological or ecclesiastical one. Indeed only under the protection of law can the free man exercise those choices of creed and worship without persecution or any other limitation of his personality. This is a position of pertinence for Christianity because any conditions which prohibit genuine choices are a serious handicap to the propagation of the Christian faith.

It may well be asked, however, whether it is possible to make a free choice in a country where one church is established by law and may be considered as the sole guardian of religious truth. Only the law can then be the guardian of conscience and choice, ensuring that, to use Lord Acton's phrase, " the co-existence of different religions is admitted with an equal right to govern themselves according to their own several principles ".[1] Where, however, an absolutist church considers itself as the sole fountain head of religious truth, then, of course, any toleration towards other groups is, in its eyes, wrong—hence the bitterness of persecution

[1] Acton, op. cit., pp. 152-3.

and the inevitability of it. Dissent then, on the highest of all counts, becomes dangerous and must be eradicated, unless the law secures freedom of religious choice and association leading to toleration.

Toleration, however, is not true liberty when it is only a gracious concession made by the state to the individual. Gracious concessions are incompatible with liberty of religion which is not something that a state, or an absolutist church, offers, but that which the citizen claims and the law protects. We have to distinguish, therefore, between "religious toleration" (something conceded) and "religious liberty" (something claimed), two notions which have characteristically been intermixed in the civil and religious contentions of Britain. A further distinction might be drawn between "freedom of religion" as concerned with rights which can be established in law, and "religious freedom" where the religious man moves in the world of duties and obligations. Both are necessary, and the test is always a practical one.

The modern requirements of religious liberty are well summed up in the *Charter of Religious Freedom* contained in *Human Rights and Religious Freedom*.[1]

1. Freedom of religion is an essential and integral aspect of human freedom. It includes the freedom of all human beings to choose for themselves their religious belief and adherence, and to change them if they so desire.

2. The rights which guarantee the full development of human beings, in the integrity and dignity of their human personality, include the religious rights not only of freedom to worship according to conscience, but also of freedom to educate, to propagate and to persuade, and to conduct social and charitable activities.

3. The rights of meeting guaranteed by a community to its members include the right of meeting for the purpose of worship according to conscience.

[1] *Human Rights and Religious Freedom*, statement issued by the Joint Committee on Religious Liberty, March 1947, pp. 4f.

4. The rights of association guaranteed by a community to its members include the right of association for religious purposes—that is to say, not only for the purpose of worship according to conscience, but also for the purposes of religious education, propagation and persuasion, and of social and charitable activities. Religious associations are accordingly free, on the same basis as other associations and subject to the same limits imposed by the necessities of public order, security and morality, to acquire and hold property, and to act generally for the fulfilment of their purposes.

5. The rights of freedom of expression of thought (by speech, writing, printing and publishing) guaranteed by a community to its members include the rights of expression of religious thought, of the propagation of religious belief, and of religious persuasion, subject to the same limits as are imposed on the general freedom of expression of thought by the necessities of public order, security and morality.

6. The rights of children to receive instruction and education with a due regard to their freedom include the right to receive religious instruction and education when such instruction and education is desired by their parents.

7. The rights of religious freedom—in meeting for worship, in association, in the expression of thought, and in instruction, education and persuasion—include the right of persons and groups to be guaranteed against legal provisions and administrative acts which are calculated to impose disabilities on grounds of religion.

This Charter was aptly summarized by the Archbishop of York in a speech in the House of Lords when he defined religious freedom as

freedom to worship according to the conscience and to bring up children in the faith of their parents; freedom for the individual to change his religion; freedom to preach, educate, publish and carry on missionary activity; and freedom to organize with others and to acquire and hold property for those purposes.[1]

[1] *Hansard*, December 4, 1946, p. 595.

III

Most of the points in this Charter will be referred to in later sections of this book. What I want to ask now is whether there is a ground for religious liberty beyond that of the positive law enacted by the state, beyond political and ecclesiastical theory and even theological argument.

In other words, is religious liberty a natural right belonging to every man because of his human nature—that law which Mr. Gladstone once called " the higher ground of natural justice, that justice which binds man to man, which is older than Christianity, because it was in the world before Christianity, because it extends to the world beyond Christianity; and which underlies Christianity, for Christianity itself appeals to it ".[1]

To define natural rights is as complicated as any attempt to define religious liberty, for (to quote Sir Ernest Barker) " few Englishmen might know what you meant if you spoke to them of natural rights, but most Englishmen believe in natural rights ".[2] There is a warmth about Cicero's classic sentence, " that we are born for justice, and that right is found not in opinion but in nature ",[3] which finds a welcome in the heart of the modern man who vaguely believes in the unwritten law—" the order of naturally sacred things ". If we argue with Maritain that " the worth of the person, his liberty, his rights, arise from the order of naturally sacred things ", then we are on higher ground still in our estimate of man as a " person who possesses absolute dignity because he is in direct relationship with the absolute in which alone he can find his complete fulfilment ".[4] Does this imply that religious liberty stands amongst the " naturally sacred things " which belong to man by natural right?

[1] Gladstone, *Speech Against the China War*, 1857 (quoted Bates 379).
[2] Ernest Barker, *Church, State and Study*, p. 155.
[3] Cicero, *De legibus*, II, 4, 10.
[4] Jacques Maritain, op. cit., p. 6.

William Penn undoubtedly believed that it did. He based his claim to liberty of conscience on " our undoubted right by the law of God, of Nature and of our country ", a natural law which presupposes " God's operations as Creator and Preserver, and thus presupposes that the created world has a structure which the Natural Law expresses ".[1] If religion is the expression of the relationship between God and man then the right of approach to God as a free man, and the right to shape this approach as a man may be guided, would appear to be among the basic facts of natural law which (to use Maritain's words) " cannot be tampered with by the state nor fall into its clutches ".[2]

The Christian philosopher goes on, of course, to find reinforcement of natural law in the Law of God and the Lordship of Jesus Christ to whom all authority in heaven and in earth has been given. Here we are on the high and massive ground of the Christian doctrine of man created in the image of God and redeemed by Christ— a teaching from which comes our belief in the equality of all men, and that each individual must be regarded as an end in himself whatever his race, colour, class or nation.[3]

Religious liberty, then, has some claim to be rooted in the natural law—the great unwritten law by which the life and being of the individual man rests finally on the eternal and sacred justice of God—a law which, for the Christian man, is reinforced by the Christian belief which links it with the Law of God whose revelation we see in Christ.

Natural law, however, or the Law of God is only capable of application as positive law, or working law, when the competent authority—whether king or legislative assembly —chooses so to apply its principles. It is then that the critical challenges arise because laws may often appear to individual men to infringe their basic rights. It may easily

[1] Quoted Bates, op. cit., p. 381.
[2] Maritain, op. cit., p. 43.
[3] Vidler and Whitehouse, *Natural Law*, pp. 23f.

be assumed, too, by the law-making body that the will of the most powerful party in the state is law without reference to natural law and the eternal Law of God. It is then the duty of the religious man—above all men—to remind the state of the ultimate origin of life and law, which he can do effectively by ensuring that amongst his general liberties this precious one of religious liberty is preserved in practice as well as in theory.

RELIGIOUS LIBERTY IN HISTORY

ON March 29, 1946, the British House of Commons had one of those debates in which it excels. It was about religion—whether or not soldiers should be compelled to attend church parades. Colonels and majors who had served in the army for thirty years and more testified to the efficacy of church parades. One brigadier even likened it to " family worship ", while another advanced the ingenious notion that some men would be too shy to attend unless they were compelled; an ex-navy man revealed that in Admiralty instructions religion came under the heading of " discipline, summary punishment "; a historian warned the House that legally everyone who was an adherent of the Church of England and did not attend divine worship on Sunday was still liable every time to a fine of five shillings. " The church can drag a seaman to the altar by a lanyard," warned a member, " but it will not make a Christian out of him by doing so." The debate was instructive, even diverting, testimony to the place of religion in British life, but as one member—Mr. Vernon Bartlett—concluded:

We are told that we fought the war in defence of the four freedoms, one of which is freedom to worship. I suggest that freedom to worship implies freedom to worship when you like, where you like and how you like; and it cannot possibly mean compulsion to worship when and where you do not like. . . . Some people believe in totalitarian systems. This compulsion to worship is a tendency in that direction. If we need that spiritual revival, the worst possible way of getting it is by compelling men in the Forces to go on church parade.[1]

[1] *Hansard*, March 29, 1946, p. 725.

Compulsory church parades[1] are a relic of the days in the history of religious liberty in the British Isles when it was thought right to compel men to attend worship, not only for the sake of religion but for the sake of civil and military obedience—a similar academic compulsion was enforced in the colleges of Oxford and Cambridge—and the disappearance of compulsion is a recognition that true religion can only flourish in freedom—truly a very modern idea.

Historically it was the Hebrew and Christian conception of a single and universal God that introduced a religious exclusivism leading to compulsion and persecution in the realm of religion. Ancient religions were regarded as confined to each separate people believing in them, and the question of change from one religious belief to another did not arise. It was not until an exclusive dogma appeared, as in Christianity, with its belief in an exclusive fellowship, that the questions of proselytism, change of belief and liberty of religion arose.

It was this exclusivism introduced into the world of the Roman Empire by early Christianity that caused the idea of religious liberty to appear for the first time. The persecution of Christians in the Empire, inspired in the first instance by considerations of public order, challenged the right to believe or not to believe. Face to face with the power of Rome, Christians were ready to make the greatest sacrifices for this new right to believe. It was this faith, officially installed by Constantine in A.D. 313 as the religion of the Empire, which gradually became intolerant of other views both within and without its borders. Both the old paganisms and the new heresies came under the official ban, and the primitive Christianity which had gloriously resisted persecution in the name of liberty of belief hardened into

---

[1] Now abolished in Navy, Army and Air Force for men of adult years.

an institution whose official agencies eradicated error and unbelief.

The Christian religion, now allied to the Empire, was used to preserve a religious unity while the ancient political unity was finally crumbling away. Religious intolerance was enthroned by the combined power of state and church, and as the secular empire faded so the empire of the Church rose in strength, competent to call for obedience in religious belief and able to enforce it by the aid of the civil power.

To look for the idea of religious liberty, or even the idea of toleration, in the Middle Ages is to look for something of which that great period of religious history had no knowledge. To maintain religious unity was the all-absorbing struggle of the Middle Ages to which priest and knight, pope and emperor were divinely dedicated. Heresy was stamped out by inquisition and the stake, and paganism itself assaulted by all the power and heroism of arms. Religious liberty and toleration were not within the vocabulary of either popular or official religion. Nor could this be wondered at in an age which viewed its mission as nothing less than the establishment of the Reign of God whose subjects had to be loyal in Christian doctrine, without taint of heresy, and who might, legitimately, be compelled to conform to Christian belief as the Church saw it.

So far from allowing variations in belief or order the medieval church quite logically conceived it to be a duty to compel all men to believe alike. Even Augustine who disliked corporal penalties in matters of belief came to hold that men may thus be brought to see the true faith, and even went to the extent of justifying himself by quoting Christ's words " Compel them to come in ".[1] An odd distortion of scripture but comforting to the medieval man who for the sake of the other man's soul was prepared to

[1] Luke xiv. 23.

25

castigate his own body if by any chance both might be saved from hell. No questioning of belief could possibly be admitted when the awful abyss of the nether-world opened for the unbeliever—to save the heretic from that by examination and torture was surely a merciful act! It justified the Holy Office of the Inquisition and made heresy detested by the masses as a rebellion against spiritual authority which might—if allowed to develop—undermine the very existence of society. Christendom was a unity, and any attempt to challenge its cohesion was a revolt. Even heretics accepted the logic of this position and would in their turn have persecuted the unbeliever! Neither the Church, jealously guarding the whole corpus of the Christian faith, nor the small sect propagating its conception of the truth, thought religious toleration desirable.

I

It was not therefore to be expected that the leaders of the Reformation could, or would, suddenly be men of religious toleration in the modern manner. It is an error in our historical estimate of that period to expect the full flower of toleration or freedom to appear miraculously. Luther and Calvin were men linked by birth and education with the Catholic tradition of medieval days, and the violence of both of them was not only characteristic of the two men but of the age which moulded them. " Heretics are not to be disputed with," said Luther, " but to be condemned unheard ", and at the hands of Calvin, Servetus—the argumentative Spaniard who held anti-Trinitarian views—died at the stake in Geneva. Calvin's own city was in its rigour and discipline a medieval community, reinforced by the doctrine of predestination, where you might be disciplined for missing the Sacraments, and punished for frivolous behaviour. In this atmosphere of intolerance the issue was obedience rather than liberty as in any un-Reformed community.

But the spirit of the Reformation as a whole inevitably worked for toleration and liberty. Where the Calvinists were in a minority in Europe they fought for freedom from state control and for freedom of worship. What they denied within their own citadel they strenuously demanded elsewhere. It was not an inconsistency, as it appears, but a shrewd recognition by Calvinism that the developing modern state had a place in human life which should be respected as long as it was used to aid the true faith and preserve liberty of worship for the elect. Calvinism in its later development, especially in Britain and America, was bound eventually to be on the side of religious liberty because of its conception of the voluntary church principle and its belief in the free community, two ideas which helped to lay the foundations of modern democracy.

Luther's vehemence against opposition to his beliefs was as violent as Calvin's, and while his rule was not so concentrated as Calvin's in Geneva his warnings to the German princes are evidence of his mind. " It will be heavy on your conscience ", he told the Duke of Saxony, " if you tolerate the Catholic worship, for no secular prince can permit his subjects to be divided by the preaching of opposite doctrines." He raged against the " Roman Sodom " who " corrupt without end the Church of God; why do we not rather assault them with all arms and wash our hands in their blood? " But even with Luther there were gleams of new understanding about religious liberty as in his famous comment on the parable of the tares:

See, then, what mad folk we have so long been, who have wished to force the Turk to the faith with the sword, the heretic with fire, and the Jews with death, to root out the tares with our own power, as if we were the people

27

who could rule over hearts and spirits and make them religious and good, which God's Word must do.[1]

Luther's wistful comment revealed a spirit totally foreign to the official religious leaders of the sixteenth century, when both Catholics and Protestants persecuted the Jews, maintained public and private inquisitions and believed that a heretic was worse than a murderer.

We must look elsewhere for more formal statements of religious liberty, and oddly enough one of them lies in that " heretical " stream of Socinianism (or Unitarianism) which beginning in the Italian Humanist movement passed into Switzerland, where Calvin condemned it as anti-Trinitarian, and then took refuge in Poland, in Holland, and finally across the seas in America. The nobility of the Socinian Catechism of Rakau (1605), with its declaration that " it is not our intention to declare war upon anybody ", is harmony amidst the clashing discords of the seventeenth century. " Why do ye not remember ", it asks, " that our only Master is Christ, and that we are all brothers, and that to none has been given power over the souls of others? If one of the brothers is more learned than the others, yet in regard to liberty and relationship with Christ all are equal."[2] The Socinians fared hard at the hands of the Reformation leaders because freedom of this kind did not hold first place in the minds of the Reformers; they were concerned about truth —and truth without dissension was an absolute necessity for the new Protestant commonwealths.

An even richer and more fruitful source of religious liberty lies in the witness of the Baptist churches whose devotion to this idea, through years of persecution in Protestant Europe, makes their place a foremost one in the history of liberty. The Baptists repudiated entirely the place of the civil power in the affairs of the Church. Churches

[1] Quoted Bates, p. 155.
[2] Ruffini, *Religious Liberty*, p. 72.

28

were spontaneous, spiritual groups in which every man was a priest and possessed the right of private judgement. John Smyth, the first English Baptist, held in his *Confession of Faith* (1611) " that the magistrate is not by vertue of his office to meddle with religion, or matters of conscience, to force and compell men to this or that form of religion, or doctrine: but to leaue Christian religion free, to euery man's conscience ".[1]

His disciple Thomas Helwys fearlessly reminded James I that he was " mortall man, and not God ", and consequently had " no power over ye immortall soules of his subjects, to make lawes and ordinances for them, and to set spirituall lords over them ". Helwys' book *The Mistery of Iniquity* (1612) broke new ground in its insistence on universal religious liberty—far ahead of its time and poignantly prophetic since through this persecuted witness the flower of liberty ultimately blossomed.

While the Reformation leaders were not so radical as the Baptist apologists they did begin processes of freedom which led, ultimately, to toleration. Liberty of judgement; the primary place of the Scriptures; a readiness to break with past traditions, and a mortal blow at the conception of a centralized authority governing the spiritual life were all part of the liberating process.

Europe had to accustom itself to the separated camps of Protestants and Catholics, discovering by tragic trial and error that religious minorities (e.g. Huguenots in France, Waldensians in Italy) could not be exterminated, and that some sort of working arrangement for toleration was necessary. In this process the rulers of the new Protestant states assisted on other grounds than religious. Peace and order were clearly preferable to religious fanaticism, and, as in England, rulers sought to impose ecclesiastical uniformity for the sake of the general welfare of their realms. The

[1] Quoted Wheeler Robinson, *The Life and Faith of the Baptists*, p. 124.

fact that they did so not on theological or religious grounds primarily, was in itself a distinct contribution to the growth of the modern view of the separation of Church and State, and towards freedom for religious groups.

When once the idea of persecution on theological grounds had been abandoned, and people dubbed " heretics " were allowed to live, it became clearer to thinking men that strict theological uniformity could not be enforced. Each man was seen to be responsible for his own soul's salvation, and hence individual religious liberty was bound to become a prized possession.

Another Reformation contribution towards religious liberty lay in the slowly dawning recognition (a process still not complete) that a claim to the exclusive possession of religious truth could not be maintained by two or more groups. What was religiously true one side of the Rhine could not be false on the other! Reasonable men came to see that religious truth was both universal and relative, and that both sides in a controversy might possess pieces of the truth, and that, at any rate, they might rejoice in their common agreements and be more charitable about their differences. This reasonable approach to religious controversy (a gift from the Humanists rather than the Fathers of the Reformation!) was only dimly apprehended in the sixteenth and seventeenth centuries, but the Reformation had unwittingly facilitated its birth. Amidst the harsh Protestant dogmas of the time, as formidably opposed to freedom of religion as any Catholic ones, this pale flower of reason and tolerance took root in a rather barren soil. It ultimately grew and flourished because it drew sustenance and life from the spirit of enquiry, experiment and reason for which the Reformation, in spite of itself, created channels all through the life of Europe.

II

While the same processes were transported across the English Channel, Britain added some all-important native contributions to the growth of religious liberty.

In Scotland Calvinism triumphed in the face of kingly divine rights and provided a turbulent and divided people with a central discipline which sharpened their desire for liberty. The enquiring spirit of reason found north of the Tweed a philosophically minded people eager for argument and naturally apt in theological dispute. While heretics might be persecuted, and the close supervision of local and national life appear to be a clamp on liberty, there were parallel forces at work which ensured freedom of the spirit. Clericalism, for instance, often a reactionary power in Protestant and Catholic Europe, was well controlled in Scotland. Laymen sat side by side in the kirk session with ministers. Democratically elected, the dour Scottish elder formed an invaluable link in the liberties of the Scottish people. Another remarkable contribution which Calvinism made to Scottish liberties was its belief in education, and its high conception of a trained ministry whose disputations and formidably composed sermons furnished the Scottish people of all sorts with an exercise ground for their shrewd and enquiring minds. In a land where philosophy was in the blood and logic an everyday occupation liberty was sure of final triumph.

When Mary Stuart tried to ban the meetings of the General Assembly of the Church of Scotland, John Knox replied, " Take from us the liberty of assemblies and take from us the Gospel." The public rights of the Church as a spiritual institution owning allegiance to no earthly ruler were fearlessly stated in Scotland. This national church, practically another name for the nation itself, might compel a uniformity of belief according to Bible standards, but there was always the element of popular consent in the compulsion. The alliance of " liberty and presbytery " was solid in the esteem of the Scottish people. Attack one and you attacked both—an attitude which served to preserve religious unity in Scotland as nowhere else.

Across the border the Reformation in England was from the first a royal, political and legal affair. The break with Rome was viewed in these terms rather than in any deeply religious ones, and religious liberty resulted only incidentally from the forces that the English Reformation let loose. Neither Henry VIII nor Elizabeth, in their attempts to provide a religious settlement for England, were concerned about religious liberty. They were determined primarily to have a single nation and a single church with the monarch as head, and a place for every Englishman within this comprehensive religious establishment.

This English ideal never became a fact, although the attempt to impose it lasted for a century and a half. During this period the foundations and forms of English religious liberty were fashioned, largely out of the very dissensions themselves, for " it was the competing claims of religious bodies ", according to J. N. Figgis, " and the inability of any single one of them to destroy the other which finally secured liberty "[1]—both political and religious.

There were in England, as Sir Ernest Barker has pointed out, two Reformations,[2] and neither of them was prepared to be tolerant towards the other. Archbishop Laud in Charles I's time laboured hard to drill the English people into uniform habits of religious belief and worship, but his failure did not prevent the Presbyterians and Independents in their hour of triumph, a few years later, trying their hand at a similar obstinate undertaking. The idea of a single

[1] J. N. Figgis, *Churches in the Modern State*, p. 101.
[2] See Bishop of Durham, *The Anglican Tradition in the Life of England*, and E. A. Payne, *The Free Church Tradition in the Life of England*.

inclusive religious society co-extensive with the nation was fiercely attractive to both Reformation traditions. Anglicanism won its partial triumph in Charles II's reign, but Puritanism remained a powerful minority in the national life, wresting its privileges of worship from an unwilling state and constituting itself a national watchdog in all matters of liberty. In this lay Puritanism's unique contribution to English life, for out of that vigilance came modern English democracy with its respect for minorities, their rights and privileges, including religious liberty.

The contemporary setting in which the practical issues of English religious liberty were faced can be followed in the great army debates, December 1648 to January 1649,[1] in which Ireton (Cromwell's son-in-law) displayed all the inbred Calvinistic fear of licence in religion whether the danger was popery, prelacy or an eccentric sect. He argued that the magistrate has no power over conscience (" if I had a thousand noes I should give it "), but he challenged the Independent divines to face gravely the implications of toleration. Was the magistrate to have no power to restrain idolatry and atheism? Was anything which called itself religion to be tolerated? In other words, how was heresy to be dealt with?

To this argument the Independents, led by John Goodwin, made an impressive answer which shows how far responsible English thought was moving in the direction of religious liberty. They argued that the spiritual persuasion of Christ alone and not the temporal ruler is effective answer in cleansing men of heresy and error. The ruler's authority was strictly civil, whereas the Kingdom of God was spiritual. If the magistrate had the power suggested then his rule was universal and infallible, and he was quite as likely to destroy good as well as evil.

At this point Cromwell himself began to take a closer

[1] See A. S. P. Woodhouse, *Puritanism and Liberty*.

C

interest in the great question. He held that all men may find God's truth and are not to be disturbed in the pursuit, a belief supported by his many acts of toleration towards individuals, including Anglicans, Presbyterians and Quakers. His belief in toleration is seen in his proclamation of 1654 summoning the nation to fasting and humiliation. He pleaded for charity and forbearance in the new attempt to gather the shattered fragments of Protestantism together. " Do not some of us affirm ourselves ", he asked, " to be the only true ministry, and true Churches of Christ, and only to have the ordinances in purity, excluding our brethren, though of equal gifts, and having as large a seal of their ministry, and desiring with as much fervour and zeal to enjoy the ordinances in their utmost purity? "[1] This large toleration would have established a loosely federated church with unofficial toleration for Anglicans, Roman Catholics, Jews and Quakers, an aim largely defeated by a parliament dominated by the sectaries which, after a dozen years of bitter storms and debate, could still argue in the *Humble Petition and Advice* that England should avoid " the permission of the exercise of more religions than one, which is a dangerous indulgence and toleration "—advice which the Protector accepted for the sake of constitutional peace, but rejected in the wide tolerance of his administration. Cromwell saw, as few of his followers did, that religious freedom was the wholly new factor in English life emerging from the revolutionary period, and that if wisely used it might be the principle of unity for diverse groups of Englishmen. His own secretary, John Milton, in the *Areopagitica*, conveys something of the spirit of Cromwellian tolerance:

A little forbearance of one another and some grain of charity might win all these diligencies to joyn and unite in one general and brotherly search after truth, could we but forgoe this prelaticall tradition of crushing free con-

[1] Quoted Jordan, Vol. III, p. 156.

sciences and Christian liberties into canons and precepts of men. . . .

Give me the liberty to know, to utter, and to argue freely according to conscience, above all liberties.

With the Restoration a fresh period of religious intolerance began, and a last attempt was made on the grand scale to force the English people into a nation-church mould. But by this time the idea of the independent church with its belief in freedom of religious association and freedom from state compulsion in religious matters had taken deep root in English life, and the repressive measures of the Clarendon Code (1661-1665) only served to inaugurate a new and vigorous nonconformity. When in 1662 two thousand Puritan clergy were expelled from their livings in the Established church for refusing to give their " unfeigned consent and assent " to everything in the prayer book, England became permanently divided between Anglicanism and Dissent, but the goal of religious liberty was brought inevitably nearer.

The Toleration Act of 1689, often described as a "curious patchwork of compromise, illogicality and political good sense ", is a landmark in the history of English religious freedom. At last the attempt, which had been made in some form or other by all religious parties during the previous hundred years, to impose a national church was abandoned, and, protected by parliamentary statute from royal, episcopal, magisterial and popular interference, Protestant Dissenters were free to develop their life. Only Unitarians and Roman Catholics were excluded, and for Protestant Dissenters themselves many civil disabilities remained.

By 1700 Englishmen had grown weary of religious controversy; the fires were burning themselves out. The influence of a philosopher like Locke, who not only advocated toleration but also separation of church and state, helped to convince men that tolerance alone—with all its risks—was the only way of controlling almost uncontrollable religious passions.

England needed unity, too, in the face of the challenges which were coming to her from the Continent, but the old idea of religious unity was clearly unattainable. The rifts were too deep and the divisions too prolonged to allow of any reconciliation—the two Reformation streams must flow on side by side with their freedom guaranteed by the state. Men also began to distinguish between what you might punish a man for, and what you might not. There was clearly punishment due for material crime and for violation of the peace, but should a man be punished for holding certain opinions? Answers to that question were practical steps on the road to religious freedom.

But although toleration was achieved, full religious equality took another two hundred years to achieve. Only gradually, and as the result of much militant pressure, were the civil and educational disabilities of Dissenters and Roman Catholics abolished. Religious tests for office and position became outmoded in a world where freedom of thought and speech were the first demands of the intelligent citizen. Having secured religious liberty by means of two revolutions England was in no mood to have a third to secure religious equality! The processes—often long and wearisome—of parliamentary legislation secured all the freedom needed for English citizens regardless of their religious professions, an achievement which, though typically English in method, became an example to the rest of the world.

III

CHRISTIANITY AND RELIGIOUS

LIBERTY

THE record of the Christian Church in relation to religious liberty is not an unblemished one of liberal toleration.

It is one of the paradoxes of Christianity that it holds within itself revolutionary teaching about liberty for the individual and what often seems to be a reactionary intolerance in dealing with the results of liberty. The Christian Gospel was preached as a message of freedom and liberty. Christ made men free from the bondage of law and gave them a new liberty as sons of God. He delivered them from the fear of death, from over-concern about daily living, and by His own life, death and resurrection provided a fresh appraisement for the life of man. It was a freedom-giving Gospel, the human soul was of immeasurable value in the sight of God, and any slight upon the most humble human being was a denial of the essential sonship between God and man. Christ Himself preached no systematic doctrine of liberty. The fact of Christian liberty arose naturally out of the new kingdom inaugurated in the Realm of God where God is the Father of all men, and the pattern of human life is based not on " rights " and " claims " but on filial relationships.

In dealing with individual men Christ was clearly on the side of an open and voluntary fellowship rather than a compulsory allegiance. There is the instance in St. Luke's Gospel where James and John ask Christ to " bid fire to come down from heaven and consume " those who refuse to receive Him[1]—a demand which Christ rejected as being alien to the spirit of His teaching. He rebuked His disciples for their suggestion, seeing in it the seeds of a persecuting spirit which was foreign to His nature and purpose.

He knew that His Kingdom could only be established upon the voluntary allegiance of men, and that no compulsion could be justified. When official Christianity has departed from this view and resorted to intolerance and persecution it has departed violently from the spirit of the Master. Much of its persecuting spirit may have appeared historically justifiable and necessary, but judged by the standards of Christ it stands condemned.

All through the New Testament the strain of intolerance is a spiritual intolerance rather than a physical one. The Christian faith was born into a world which was hostile to a belief claiming such high authority and such exclusive attributes. Christ Himself criticized the prevailing religious system of His day with epithets such as " blind guides ", "hypocrites", and with a condemnation of those who made void the Word of God because of their traditions. He was stern and unsparing of those in official religious positions who abused their positions and privileges for their own ends, and wherever He saw power being used unintelligently He withered it with scorn. But His weapons were words. There is no hint in His teaching that the new belief should be imposed on unwilling minds by force. He used satire, scorn, argument, appeals to conscience and solemn warnings of judgement to come, but there was no suggestion that His followers should regard themselves as instruments of God's judgement.

No one in the New Testament is more outspoken about false doctrine and false teachers than St. Paul. He warns his friends in the churches of " false apostles, deceitful workers, fashioning themselves into apostles of Christ ",[1] and against " the enemies of the Cross of Christ, whose end is perdition, whose god is the belly, who mind earthly things ".[2] In his letters to Timothy his young colleague is advised to " take heed to thyself and to thy doctrine ";[3] to " charge certain men not to teach a different doctrine ",[4] and to guard his flock against the evils of the " hypocrisy of men that speak lies, branded in their conscience as with a hot iron ".[5] All the apostle's censures are directed against the character of the false teachers coupled with a warning to his hearers and correspondents not to be misled by them.

In the Epistle to the Galatians St. Paul deals with teaching directly contrary to the faith he was advocating. He meets the attempts of the Judaisers to contract Christianity into a sect of their faith with fierce denunciation, and insists that what has happened in Jesus Christ is a new event in religious history, and defends his own position as an apostle with strong personal feeling. But there are no hints or threats of persecution against the Judaisers. On the contrary, the apostle argues that the Jewish system must be tested by its own fruits in the same way as Christianity. The only demand he makes is that the new faith shall be given freedom to grow and develop and not be brought back again into the bondage of the law.

This spiritual liberty is the birthright of the Christian believer, who accepts the lordship of Christ—that is the apostle's thesis all through the significant pages of the Galatian epistle. From the bondage of " the law " the new man in Christ is delivered into a new relationship with God where such problems as circumcision, the sabbath and its ritual, and the minute observances of the law are removed from the shoulders of the believer. He puts on a living garment of faith which supplants the rigorous casing of the

---

[1] 2 Cor. xi. 13. [2] Phil. iii. 18-19. [3] 1 Tim. iv. 16.
[4] ibid., i. 3. [5] ibid., iv. 2.

law-regime. He is a member of a new humanity which transcends all racial superiority and is inclusive of diverse cultures and national allegiances. The Christian stands amongst a re-born citizenry, who have freedom as their birthright. Paul was proud of his Jewish heritage which he regarded as being fulfilled in Christ, and all he asked of his Galatian friends was liberty for the new faith. There was no compulsion to believe and no uniformity demanded of the Christian believer—except the uniformity of sincerity.

The test of sincerity seems to be the one universal New Testament test. Any other imperfections of faith, knowledge or love could be remedied by the working of the Spirit, but the elementary condition of sincerity was the essential foundation of the Christian life. Apostolic denunciations, which wax louder and sharper towards the end of the New Testament, are all charged with the dangers of paganism, profligacy of all sorts, sins of the flesh and the poisoning of the pure stream of the faith by the infiltration of pagan customs—but the Truth is powerful enough to deal with them all.

This Christian truth and its revelation in Christ are for the Christian man the foundation of his belief in liberty. For him Christian liberty is a religious experience, a direct consequence of his personal faith in God. No state or other authority may stand between him and God, or attempt to control the intimate relationship between the human soul and its Maker. The answer of Peter and John in Acts iv. 19, " whether it be right in the sight of God to hearken unto you rather than unto God, judge ye " has been echoed in all the great contentions about Christian liberty. New Testament Christianity clearly established a personal relationship between God and man to which a man must respond for himself. Liberty is born out of this experience. The " new man in Christ " is the centre-piece of the New Testament teaching about liberty for, to use the words of

John Smyth, the Baptist pioneer, " Christ onlie is the King, and law giver of the Church and conscience ".[1]

I

However much official Christianity may have departed from the New Testament teaching, it has always re-discovered there the basis of Christian belief in the supremacy of the individual personality. Personal liberty for the Christian is rooted in his belief in God and Christ's revelation of the nature of God. That for him is part of the nature of ultimate reality, and it is there that personal liberty finds its origin. If the Christian faith is the ultimate truth about God and man then the sanctity of human personality and the liberties which go with it are sustained by the Christian faith, and if that is denied then liberty itself disappears.

The New Testament and the Christian faith in history are witnesses to the freedom conferred on man by the Christian revelation—a fact rarely recognized except at moments of contemporary crisis as in Western Europe at the present time, when the foundations of liberty and the meaning of man and his place in ordered community life are up for judgement. It is Christianity's great achievement that it has woven its belief in the sanctity of human personality and the liberty of the individual man into the conscience of Western Europe. If no single nation has fully translated this Christian teaching into its practical way of life, the general conscience of Western European thought has been quickened and irrigated by the doctrine. Liberty of conscience, liberty of speech, and liberty of association (not always actively promoted by official Christianity) find their true home and source in God's view of man as seen in Christ's revelation. Religious liberty is clearly linked with

[1] Wheeler Robinson, op. cit., p. 124.

41

these general liberties, and it cannot logically be separated out from amongst them.

The importance of this link was stressed by James Harrington during the vital seventeenth-century debates in England when he remarked that " without liberty of conscience civil liberty cannot be perfect; and without civil liberty liberty of conscience cannot be perfect ".[1] The English achievement of civil and religious liberties shows that the two are mightily linked together, and that a threat to one means a threat to the other. John Milton, too, believed that a free commonwealth in which civil liberty was already established would be more likely than any other government to favour and protect " this liberty of conscience, which above all other things ought to be to all men dearest and most precious ".[2]

How vital the link is to-day may be seen in these two comments on Russia and Germany. Writing in the *New York Times*, in October 1941, on religious liberty in Russia, Anne McCormick says:

> Stalin cannot reverse the fixed policy of more than twenty years and allow not merely freedom of worship, which exists in Russia in the sense that churches are still open, but freedom to teach religion, without opening the way to other revolutionary changes. For liberty, like peace and war, is indivisible. It is impossible to grant freedom of worship without granting freedom of speech, freedom of the press, freedom of assembly. Religious liberty cannot exist without civil liberty and vice versa.

And this from a German Catholic Pastoral letter of March 22, 1942:

> We wish particularly to stress that we are not only standing up for religious and ecclesiastical rights, but also for the ordinary rights of mankind. Every honour-

---

[1] Quoted Jordan, op. cit., Vol. IV, p. 289.
[2] Milton, *The Ready and Easy Way*, p. 34. (E. M. Clark's edition.)

able man is interested in the respect and maintenance of these rights; without them the whole of Western culture must collapse. We definitely and firmly refuse the demand that we should show our loyalty to our country by being faithless to Christ and our Church. . . . We keep faith at any price with God and our Church.[1]

While it is true that religious liberty has not been (as is popularly supposed) the first liberty to flourish in the modern state, the struggle for religious tolerance has been a major force working for general liberty in Western Europe. In their witness against state absolutism both the Roman Catholic and Protestant churches helped to preserve the integrity of the individual conscience, but paradoxically there is also plenty of evidence that official Roman Catholic action has often been against liberty and democracy, and that the submissiveness of Lutherans and Anglicans to state authority enabled their churches to be used to retard the growth of liberty.

The complicated and paradoxical part played by official Christianity in the growth of religious liberty is sufficient warning to the Christian man not to overstate his claim (as is frequently done) that religious liberty is the mother of all other liberties. The development of religious toleration in England alone is sufficient warning that, far from being the earliest liberty, religious liberty was the slowest liberty to develop and flourish. Magna Carta, the growth of Law and Parliament, the Petition of Right and the Bill of Rights, all came in English history before the achievement of religious toleration. Commenting on this Luzzatti, the Italian historian, remarks that " religious liberty is the most difficult and slowest of liberties to root itself in private life and in the life of the state, and while it ought to be the very basis of a civic community, generally succeeds in being only its crowning feature ".[2]

---

[1] Hugh Martin (ed.), *Christian Counter-Attack*, p. 30.
[2] Luzzatti, *God in Freedom*, p. 6.

II

How and why did the Christian Church depart from the simplicities of its early days in relation to liberty of opinion?

The answer is the long and entangled relationships between church and state which began with the official recognition of Christianity in A.D. 313 by the Emperor Constantine. That act brought Christianity into a sphere which was not its own creation, and it paid a big price for its new status backed by the massive organization of the Roman state, which had tried in vain to crush it. Paganism was forbidden, and heretics were rendered obedient by the strong arm of the law. Heresy became a crime against civil society which punished it by death. The attitude of the New Testament in commending truth by persuasion was superseded by the powerful contention of the state that truth, if it be truth, must be enforced and all brought to believe it.

The close alliance of church and state, which persisted for the thousand years and more from Constantine, and the eventual triumph of the Church equipped with the ritual and power of the decayed Roman state is the history of Western Christendom. Within that partnership the Church organized for its believers a theory of discipline and penance, and for the non-believer—or holder of erroneous opinions—persecution and punishment. The ecclesiastical system—like civil society—was served by courts, judges and executioners. As a world power the Church was thus equipped to face the devil and all his works, and in defence of the truth the Church was arguably right in suppressing error by force.

Persecution for religious opinions, held contrary to official church teaching, became an accepted part of the medieval ecclesiastical pattern and was carried over in the early Reformation period. Persecution and force were used as well to bolster up the ecclesiastical machine, and consequently the state was swift to use this strong arm for secular policies. There is no doubt that the Spanish Inquisition was used by the Spanish monarchy to weld its turbulent peoples into some sort of unity, and that the persecution in Bohemia upheld domination over the Czechs, in the same way that the religious war against the Albigensians strengthened the French monarchy.

These are hard facts which anyone discussing the relationship of Christianity and liberty must be ready to admit. Christianity had departed from its early simplicities. However much persecution theories may be justified by the turbulence of the time, the high issues at stake and the fight for the very life of the Christian faith in the Middle Ages, they are a historic liability for the Christian faith.

A. J. Carlyle, writing of the medieval period, says:

> It is unhappily true that the Christian Church, not the Christian religion . . . forgot its own doctrine that the individual was responsible only to God in spiritual things. St. Augustine's unhappy defence of the persecution of those who differed from the Church was not indeed the sole cause of this, but it contributed much to it, as we can see from the treatment of religious persecution in the Canon Law.
>
> The Church did indeed in some sense defend spiritual liberty, that is its own independence, from the authority of the Temporal Power, but it did this only to put it more completely under the control of the Church itself. This is true not only of the medieval Church, but of the Reformed Churches. It was not till the eighteenth and nineteenth centuries that the Western world recovered from this ruinous error.[1]

But the same writer, while admitting the inactivity of the Christian Church on behalf of social and political liberty during the eighteenth and nineteenth centuries, believes that Christian truth nas " recognized that the rationale of all

[1] A. J. Carlyle, *Political Liberty*, p. 204.

authority is in the end nothing but the maintenance of a righteous order ", and this fact " did render an immense service to the progress of liberty ", and that " the Church has still an important part to play in vindicating this conception of the nature of the authority of society against some mischievous and dangerous political tendencies of the modern world ".[1]

These observations sum up the strength and the weakness historically of the Christian position in relation to liberty. On the one hand, by its own Gospel, the Christian faith is committed to proclaim liberty, but on the other, its cramping alliances, particularly with the state, have promoted theories of persecution which have often made Christianity liberty's formidable opponent.

The Roman Catholic theory of compulsion and persecution[2] proceeds logically from its view of the Church as the receiver and giver of truth, and its recognition that authority resides in a definite group of persons. Continuity of authority—the essence of the compulsive attitude—is visibly provided for in Catholicism—no sinner, unbeliever or heretic may escape the long arm of ecclesiastical authority. Within the Roman church (according to its modern apologists) there is an abundance of private tolerance, mutual forbearance and respect for the individual personality and judgement of men, and in our time Western Christendom has seen an ample display of Roman Catholic opposition to the totalitarian claims of the state, in defence of Christian freedom.

Protestantism, although its Reforming fathers were as zealous and compulsive as any Catholic in control over conduct and belief, had not got the central and continuous authority necessary for really effective persecution. The Protestant theory of the Church did not grant to any one,

[1] Carlyle, *The Christian Church and Liberty*, p. 73.
[2] See " Roman Catholic position ", p. 104.

or any group of people, the final authority to compel, and although in Protestant states the secular arm was frequently used to compel belief, the Reformation fathers, in spite of inconsistencies, believed that truth alone could finally dispel error.

It may fairly be claimed by Protestantism that its belief in toleration and religious liberty grew because they were seen to be essential attributes of Christianity, for, in the main, it was the freedom of the Christian man which the Reformation re-discovered. The incompatibility of the persecuting spirit with the Spirit of Jesus; the sacredness of conscience and the view that (in the words of John Donne) " nothing hinders our own salvation more than to deny salvation to all but ourselves ",[1] all combined to inspire within the Protestant churches a love of liberty and religious freedom which was slow in many countries to assert itself in face of state and ecclesiastical authority, but which has been a major contribution to the growth and power of Christianity.

It was the Baptist Roger Williams, from his vehement citadel of freedom in New England, who put the position naïvely but concisely:

> (1) *God* requireth not an *uniformity* of Religion to be *inacted* and *inforced* in any *Civill* state; which inforced *uniformity* (sooner or later) is the greatest occasion of *civill Warre, ravishing of conscience, persecution of Christ Jesus* in his servants, and of the *hypocrisie* and destruction of millions of souls. (2) It is the will and command of *God*, that . . . a *permission* of the most *Paganish, Jewish, Turkish or Anti-christian consciences* and *worships*, bee granted to *all* men in all *Nations* and *Countries,* and they are onely to bee *fought* against with that *Sword of God's Spirit*, the *Word of God.* (3) True *civility* and *Christianity* may both flourish in a state or *Kingdome,* notwithstanding the *permission* of divers and contrary *consciences,* either to *Jew or Gentile.*[2]

[1] Donne, *Fifty Sermons*, 285.   [2] Quoted Bates, p. 427.

Williams's second contention is at the heart of the Christian teaching about liberty—there must be freedom for all religions and for those who profess no religion. Although Christianity is essentially an intolerant religion in the sense that it believes the revelation of God in Christ is universal, and that ultimately all men will bow the knee to Him who is Lord of heaven and earth, it asks for no special privileges in lands where other religions are powerfully established. The "most paganish, Jewish, Turkish or anti-Christian consciences" are only to be fought against with the "Sword of God's Spirit", and there must be freedom for all, both to preach and persuade.

Respect for the inner integrity of the other person and his rights of honest thought, and a concern for his spiritual growth are fundamental to the Christian religion. Christianity cannot deny to other faiths what it desires for itself in the field of liberty. It must be on its guard lest any doctrine of absolutes in ecclesiastical decisions, or in the formulation of dogma, should stultify the workings of conscience or deal harshly with the genuinely disturbed mind.

Christianity can best display its belief in freedom and show itself a worthy keeper of it by humility in holding the truth, and being the challenger of oppression, civil and ecclesiastical. Only in ways like these can Mandell Creighton's judgement be sustained that liberty "is always unsafe in the world and is only secure under the guardianship of the Church; for the Church possesses the knowledge of man's eternal destiny—which alone can justify his claim to freedom".[1]

III

This view of the Church is easily open to the taunts of its critics, because an intolerant exclusiveness within the Christian Church has been a source of weakness in the Christian

[1] Creighton, *Persecution and Tolerance*, p. 140.

faith and the origin of nearly all the bad relationships between religious bodies. The denial of liberty has been the breeding-ground of distrust and suspicion which in their turn have brought discredit on the whole cause of religion.

Questions which affect the relationships of religious bodies are usually ones of simple tolerance.

Is it possible, for instance, for the religiously convinced to be tolerant? Can a religious body which believes it has the truth necessary to save men afford to tolerate error? Upon questions of this kind have been built theories of persecution translated into practice by men belonging to all sections of the Christian religion. Religious liberty has often meant liberty to believe as those in authority believed, an intolerance of spirit which has happily disappeared in many lands but is liable to a resurgence where a dominant religion wields authority.

Religious bodies, too, have learned through bitter experience that the liberal temper is the only one to exercise in religious controversy, and that truth provides its own protection as long as it is allowed freedom of expression. Commenting on this point from the standpoint of the Church of England, Dr. Cecilia M. Ady, in her book *The English Church and How it Works*, says:

> The conviction that suppression of opinion does not serve the cause of religious truth, and that error can most effectively be combated if it is allowed free expression, has become a guiding principle of its official action. . . . But refusal to condemn is not to approve. By its reluctance to commit itself to doctrinal definitions, and its refusal to engage in heresy-hunting, the Church has done much to create an atmosphere in which the search for truth can proceed unhindered. It has made it possible for errors to die through their failure to convince, instead of being driven underground by suppression or fortified by the proscription of those who maintain them.[1]

[1] pp. 280-1.

D

That is a lesson which may fairly be claimed to have been learned and accepted by the Protestant, but not by the Roman Catholic, section of Christendom, whose systematic teaching hardly makes for tolerance. There are some refreshing examples of the personal recognition of tolerance by leaders of the Roman church but none which indicates an official change. Macaulay once re-stated a phrase of Augustine's[1] which crisply sums up the Roman Catholic position in relation to other religious bodies: " I am in the right, and you are in the wrong. When you are the stronger, you ought to tolerate me, for it is your duty to tolerate truth. But when I am the stronger, I shall persecute you, for it is my duty to persecute error."[2] This sounds impertinent if not hypocritical, but it is a position from which the Roman church has never retreated although under state action she has been compelled to live at peace with other religious bodies.[3]

With liberty of its own administration guaranteed by the state, it is the duty of a religious body to live at peace with other religious bodies and to respect the warning of Locke that " the arms by which the members of this society (the church) are to be kept within their duty are exhortations, admonitions and advice ". This warning applies in particular to the freedom belonging to the individual member of a religious body to change his allegiance without restraint or hindrance. Religious liberty belongs to the individual within a religious community as well as to the community itself, and the individual's right of conscience to change his own allegiance and to persuade others to do likewise must be an inviolable one.

[1] Original quoted on p. 104.
[2] Macaulay, *Essays, Sir James Mackintosh.*
[3] See pp. 106ff.

IV

RELIGIOUS LIBERTY TO-DAY—

A SURVEY

I THE CHALLENGE TO IT

IT is frequently asserted that the Atlantic Charter of August 14, 1941 (signed only by Mr. Roosevelt and Mr. Churchill), mentions religious liberty. There is no such reference in any of its eight clauses. A few months before the Charter, however, President Roosevelt, on January 6, 1941, in his Four Freedoms speech, said, "The second is freedom of every person to worship God in his own way everywhere in the world." Then, on January 1, 1942, twenty-six nations signed at Washington a Declaration which included the phrase " complete victory over their enemies is essential to defend life, liberty, independence and religious freedom ". In June 1942 President Roosevelt, in a broadcast speech to the occupied countries of Europe, referred again to " freedom of religion ", and on June 26, 1945, at San Francisco, the United Nations Charter was signed which includes the following section amongst the purposes and principles of the United Nations:

To achieve international co-operation in solving international problems of an economic, social, cultural, or humanitarian character, and in promoting and encouraging respect for human rights and for fundamental freedoms for all without distinction as to race, sex, language, or religion.[1]

These various declarations make no attempt to define

[1] *The Charter of the United Nations*, Article 1, section 3.

51

religious freedom, and one of them, President Roosevelt's famous Four Freedoms speech, is content with the phrase "freedom of worship". No doubt, President Roosevelt would probably have agreed with the wide interpretation given to religious liberty in this book. Freedom of worship is only part of that liberty. If that alone had been at stake in the Nazi regime in Germany, or in Japan, then the Christian Church would have had little to be worried about. Freedom of worship was theirs. Hitler and the Nazi philosophers, who supplied his regime with refurbished pagan doctrines, would have been quite content if the German Christians had been willing to equate freedom of religion with freedom of worship. The issue between them was more subtly threatening to the Christian Church. The question was whether worship and the observance of the sacraments had any significance for the common life, whether they had implications about race theories, state plans and policies, how men lived and what claims the state had on them. In other words, had Christianity any claim to be a religion for the whole of life or was it merely a set of ceremonies which were piously observed in the same manner as their pagan ancestors placated the gods? Freedom of worship might be granted, but freedom of religion, if it meant any sort of challenge to the state, was another matter. That the Nazis themselves realized this as well as the resolute leaders of the Confessional church is illustrated by the directives which the Gestapo issued to its agents in 1933 to guide them in their attitude to the Protestant churches:

(1) Efforts must be made to penetrate the circles of the Provisional Church Administration and the Lutheran Council with V-men;
(2) also to plant V-men in all provincial churches and in all central offices of the religious societies and agencies in your territory;

(3) further, to be oriented at all times regarding the incumbents of all the church offices;

(4) to determine the relative strength, as much as possible by statistics, or single groups;

(5) to ascertain, by an occasional check of church attendances, the interest of the population in church life;

(6) to be in possession of a church directory and to scrutinize the magazine *Junge Kirche*, also official bulletins and the most important Sunday church paper;

(7) to probe the church-political attitude of the theological faculty in each university, its measure of influence on the other faculties and the attitude of individual professors;

(8) to watch the radio programmes, theatres and movies for possible Protestant influence;

(9) to be informed regarding all Inner Mission institutions and church societies in your area, and to expose, in co-operation with the National Socialist Welfare Agency, unsanitary conditions in hospitals, etc.

(10) to investigate residence halls, student homes, confessional seminaries and Protestant homes for political attitudes and possible incidents involving paragraph 175 (i.e. sexual irregularity);

(11) to observe church methods of attracting members from the Labour Service.[1]

This was the organized opposition which faced the German churches and threatened their religious liberty. This is no place to follow in detail the ebb and flow of attack and counter-attack in recent German church history, and we can only salute in passing the gallant pastors and laymen who suffered in the concentration camps for the freedom of the Gospel. Their suffering was endured essentially for religious liberty. While the gospel of Nazism, with its abhorrent theories of race and blood, with an all-powerful state dictatorship, was the immediate cause of their perse-

---

[1] S. Herman, *The Rebirth of the German Church*, p. 67.

cutions, the underlying reason was the inability of the Nazis to endure a church whose liberty was founded in a divine order, and whose authority came from outside the state.

The challenge of the modern totalitarian state to religious liberty is the most far-reaching one. A doctrine which erects a " church-state " assumes for itself control of this most intimate and fundamental liberty. All general liberties of action, association and speech are in its keeping, and religion becomes a state worship with the ultimate obliteration of any religious relationship between an " outside deity " and the individual believer.

Undoubtedly the leaders of the Russian revolution believed that religion was, in Lenin's phrase, " an aspect of spiritual oppression ", and that it should be rooted out for the good of the state and the people. A Communist Party Programme still quotes Article 13 which was printed in 1919:

As regards religion the Party does not satisfy itself with decreeing the already separated church from state and school from church, i.e. measures which bourgeois democracy present in their programmes, but nowhere in the world has carried through to the end, thanks to the varied actual connection of capital with religious propaganda. The All-Union Communist Party directs itself by the conviction that only the realization of rational planning and conscious action in all public-economic activity of the masses will result in the complete dying out of religious prejudices. The Party strives for the complete destruction of the connection between the exploiting classes and the organizations of religious propaganda, aiding the actual release of the working masses from religious prejudice, and organizing the very broadest scientific enlightenment and anti-religious propaganda. However, it is necessarily careful to avoid any offence to the feelings of believers, leading only to the strengthening of religious fanaticism.[1]

[1] Quoted Madras Reports, Vol. VI, *The Church and the State*, p. 249.

The *Agitator's Guide*, still sold in large numbers in the Soviet Union, had these paragraphs in its May 1937 No. 8 edition:

Religion at its very roots is inimical to science. It teaches man to have blind faith and not to study, not to carry on research. Religion gives the believer a wrong, distorted conception of reality. The origin of the universe, of life on earth, of man, of mind—all this is wrongly, anti-scientifically, primitively explained in religious books. Religion holds man in darkness and ignorance.

Religion teaches that true human happiness is not on earth, but " in heaven ", that earthly life is simply a stage to the attainment of happiness after death. In order to procure " eternal bliss " after death, believing workers, according to religious teaching, must uncomplainingly carry their " cross " on earth. Patience, humility, love of enemies—these are the rules of conduct recommended to workers by religious " morality ".

Every religion brings harm to workers. . . . Lenin taught that the more refined the religion, the more harmful it became, because the more difficult for believing workers to comprehend its reactionary rôle. . . . No matter how churchmen and sectarians greet and praise the Soviet power, no matter how they try to " adjust " their " gods " to Communism, the essence of religious activity is profoundly reactionary and at its root inimical to socialism.[1]

While the doctrine that religion is harmful may be officially still held in the Soviet Union, in practice religious associations have a large amount of freedom. In the decrees of 1918 separating Church and State there are these three clauses:

Within the confines of the Republic it is prohibited to issue any local laws or regulations restricting or limiting freedom of conscience, or establishing privileges or preferential rights of any kind based upon the religious confession of the citizen.

[1] ibid., pp. 252f.

A free performance of religious rites is guaranteed as long as it does not interfere with public order, and is not accompanied by interference with the rights of citizens of the Soviet Republic. Local authorities possess the right in such cases to adopt all necessary measures to preserve public order and safety.

The school is separated from the church. Instruction in religious doctrine is not permitted in any governmental or common schools, nor in private educational institutions where general subjects are taught. Citizens may give or receive religious instruction in a private manner.[1]

Religious organizations (i.e. churches) in the Soviet Union are recognized primarily as local associations for the conduct of religious worship, and every visitor to Russia remarks on the crowded churches. One visitor to the Baptist church, off the Petrovski Boulevard, Moscow, in 1946, says:

It was packed as I have never seen a church packed before. Through the crowds which overflowed into the street we were escorted to the corner of a small gallery, from which we could look down on the throng below. I have never seen anything like it. People were standing five deep in the aisles, and on every available inch of floor space, even under the pulpit and round the chancel. The building was literally packed from wall to wall and through the open doors and vestibules. I estimated that at least 1,200 people were crowded into a church built for 500, and the service lasted two and a half hours. The building was a replica of many of the larger and old-fashioned free churches to be found in England, especially in East Anglia and the Midlands, plain and rectangular with long, clear glass windows—pulpit on one side and choir on the other, with a shallow semi-circular chancel in the centre, and on the walls (facing the congregation) large illuminated Scripture texts of the same type as one can find in most village chapels at home. The communion table was in the centre and was laden with communion cups and plates; in front was a huge

[1] Quoted Madras Reports, op. cit., p. 242.

loaf, and round the chancel sat the solemn-faced deacons. It reminded me of the strict Baptist church which I attended as a boy.[1]

In June 1942 there were over four million members of the All-Union Baptist Council. There are also 22,000 active Orthodox churches in the Union as against 4,225 in 1941. In 1945 the Patriarchate of Moscow was allowed to be re-established, with the right of operating a banking account and holding property and printing presses. Over 800 churches and ninety monasteries have been re-opened with the help of the government. Clergymen have been liber ated from the obligation for military service and monks are exempt from the bachelor tax. Special services may be held for women and children, and Christian instruction may be given to children in preparation for communion.

All this is a great advance on previous restrictive laws, and much of it is due to the general goodwill which priests and church people won during the war period. There was a return to religion in those years of strain which may herald much good for the future. But it would be mis-reading the religious situation in the Soviet Union to claim for it complete religious liberty. In administration, for instance, the Bureau of Religious Affairs appears to be the official body which has the deciding word in every new undertaking. The All-Union Council of Religious Cults is the state link with the evangelical churches and the Council for the Orthodox church with the Orthodox church. Finan-cially independent of the state the churches are said to collect money easily, but no doubt they have to render account to the Bureau about the way they spend it. Free to train a ministry, church seminaries and monasteries are open to inspection by Bureau officials. Freedom of wor-ship, association, and travel (within the Union) are recog-nized, but any ecumenical fellowship with other national

---

[1] *World Dominion*, January-February 1947, pp. 11f.

churches is almost impossible. Only limited periods of instruction for children are recognized, and there is no evidence that the distribution of the Bible is encouraged. Further, any criticism of state action by the churches would probably not be permitted. The air of liberty which churches in Western democracies breathe is absent in the Soviet Union. This is not because of any desire to persecute or abolish organized religion, but because the comprehensive state plan for the citizen's life sees religion as something conferred and guaranteed by the state at its pleasure, but without an autonomous divine life of its own. The religious life undoubtedly is followed in the Soviet Union with devotion and much selflessness, worship is free, and the growing activities of the Church are attracting many to take an interest in religious things. But all this appears to the outside observer to be at the pleasure of the state and at its best only a very limited freedom, and one which might with a change of official policy be quickly re-channelled or suspended.

In an interview (reported in a British monthly news letter)[1] Mr. George Karpov, vice-chairman of the Council for the Affairs of the Orthodox Church, said that in the Soviet Union all religious bodies had equal rights. His council " existed to ensure freedom for the Orthodox Church ", and since its foundation on October 8, 1943, it had provided an adequate link between the Patriarch and the Synod on the one hand, and the government on the other, for questions where government decisions had to be taken. " Real freedom for the church ", he said, " must mean freedom of activity for the headquarters of religious bodies, freedom to publish literature, freedom to train clergy and must include adequate facilities for religious ceremonies. . . . The state helps the church by securing supplies of wood, glass, stone and other building materials,

[1] *Religion and the People*, September 1946.

which are supplied at state prices and not at commercial prices. The same is true of cloth for robes, linen and blankets for the seminaries, for car petrol, wine, wax, paper and other commodities." Mr. Karpov said that he had received hundreds of letters thanking him for the work of the Council which had straightened out many administrative tangles and made the working of the Church easier—" the Council did not in any way interfere with the internal life of the church ".

Reliable evidence about religious liberty in the Russian dominated portions of Europe—the Baltic States, Poland, Yugo-slavia and the Balkan countries—is not so readily procurable. According to the Vatican Radio out of 1,916 parish priests in Yugo-slavia in 1939 there remain only 401; 186 have been executed without trial; 32 have been tried and then executed; 85 have been imprisoned for life; 409 have been forced into exile, and 800 are unaccounted for. Archbishop Stepinac is in prison, all religious instruction is forbidden in schools, and Roman Catholic youth movements are prohibited. A policy of antagonism to the Roman Catholic church is obviously the inspiration of many anti-religious acts in Eastern Europe.

1

The third big world challenge to religious liberty (and one which will be referred to again in later sections) is that of Islam—the world's most complete church-state system. Orthodox Islam recognizes no division between " church " and " state ", and as the law of Islam (sharia) affects the lives of millions of people in the world, this theocratic view is a formidable problem for religious liberty. In the strictest sense the question of religious liberty does not arise for the Moslem within the world of Islam, as all the faithful are within the one community moulded in the one religious and political system. To be an apostate from it is an act worthy of death, a sentence still carried out in Central Arabia and Afghanistan.

Islamic countries have been compelled, however, to face the issue of non-Moslem religiou. communities living within their borders. There are the ancient Coptic and Armenian churches, which have miraculously survived centuries of Islamic cultural and economic pressure, and during the last hundred years the missionary expansion of the Christian churches has added other communities. Islamic methods of recognition have always been those of a master towards an inferior, an attitude well summed up by Sir Charles Eliot in his book *Turkey in Europe*: "By tolerating the Christian religion, the conqueror implied that Christians were allowed to preserve not only their religion in the strict sense of the word, but all their observances, usages and customs, provided they clearly understood that they were collectively and individually the inferiors of Moslems, and paid tribute in humble gratitude for the privilege of being allowed to exist."[1]

Islam has found it useful to come to terms with "the infidel" for purposes of trade, cultural relations and for the services of education and health which missionary organizations in particular have provided, but in the main the general attitude has not fundamentally changed. Modifying influences have been at work in nearly all Islamic countries, notably in Turkey, Egypt and Iran, produced by the spread of Western influences particularly in education and social services. Islam has been shaken during the last thirty years by forces outside itself, while within its own borders every Islamic state has to contend with the force of nationalism.

Has all this contributed to religious liberty? Only general answers can be given because each Islamic country

[1] Madras Reports, Vol. VI, p. 71.

has a different way of solving the " religious minorities " problem. But in the main the solution consists of granting " community rights " to people of other religions, with freedom of worship and the right to hold property and conduct schools and hospitals. Everyone nurtured in the Western traditions of liberty knows that this is not liberty but merely a condescending offer from the majority to the minority. This freedom is granted almost in the manner of a charity, and does not belong to the citizen as an inherent right. Although international agreements such as the Lausanne Treaty (1923) and the Montreux Conference (1937) guaranteed the rights of minority communities (in Turkey and Egypt), those communities are constantly made aware of their existence on sufferance in the midst of a people where only Moslems enjoy the full rights of citizenship.

In its present structure orthodox Islam is utterly opposed to religious liberty. It has, however, shown powers of adaptation in the past, and as the independent nations of Islamic religion and culture develop their relationship with Western nations truer ideas of liberty may spread. At the moment a powerful drive of totalitarian nationalism is gathering force, and Islam is thereby nationally strengthened in the esteem of the younger generation who associate other religions (especially Christianity) with a " foreignness " which is doubly hateful. No area in which religious liberty is threatened is more crowded than the world of Islam with the problems of all kinds which the denial of liberty throws up. Some of them are mentioned in the succeeding pages. Taken together they are a formidable challenge to liberty as Western nations know it and in particular to Christianity itself.

2

Religious liberty, as has been pointed out, cannot be

separated from the general rights of man which are being threatened on a world-wide scale to-day. The ending of the war and the defeat of certain forms of totalitarianism does not end the peril. Indeed U.N.O., in one of its first acts, has set up a Commission on Human Rights which may produce an International Bill of Rights. Many feel that the time has come for an international organization, comparable to the International Labour Organization, called the Human Rights Organization, which should be regarded as an essential part of the United Nations machinery for peace.

The threat of the omni-competent state to human liberties always remains a lively possibility, and although religious liberty, as defined in this book, is the most fundamental of all liberties, it does not at once receive the recognition that is its due. Writing on this point in *The Times*, Sir Ernest Barker said:

> The passion of ideologies, the passion of nationalism, and the general surge of emotions stirred by the war and still uneasily heaving, all tend to cloud the idea of religious liberty and to make the path of religious minorities difficult. The very passion for liberty itself, if it be felt (as it tends to be) with a particular reference to politics, may obscure the idea of liberty in its reference and relation to the sphere of religion. There is still reason for proclaiming the principle that liberty is a matter of religion as well as of politics, and for vindicating the cause of " civil and religious liberty ".[1]

This lack of appreciation of the central place of religious liberty is an aspect of the general weakening of religious sanctions in every part of the world. It is also perhaps an indication that those bred in the Western tradition of Christian civilization too readily assume that all is well because they themselves experience no particular national

[1] *The Times*, August 16, 1946.

prohibition. This ostrich-like attitude is dangerous to religious liberty because this is a universal liberty. Many would regard it as the chief of liberties without which no man, whatever his race or creed, is really free. We are particularly our brother's keeper in the matter of religious liberty, and any threat to it is a threat to all who believe, whatever their belief is.

Religious liberty naturally engenders loyalties which make the state suspicious of its high claims, and it is just here that the clash is bound to come. For the Christian man with his loyalty to the Lordship of Christ and his loyalty to the state, the issue is a sharp one, and recent history has shown that there is no way out by compromise when religious liberty is challenged. The Church and her individual members must be prepared to suffer for this liberty or else surrender their very belief in all that it means. As Dr. Oldham pointed out in preparation for the Oxford Conference in 1937, " the problem is how to secure acknowledgment of the unique position of the State as the bond which holds the community together, as the representative of the whole society, as the guardian of the law and as responsible for fostering the good life of the community in all its aspects, and at the same time to bring it about that the authority of the State will be used not to suppress and limit, but to serve, promote and multiply freedom ".[1] Religious liberty is a touchstone of state action and a test by which all other liberties may be measured.

There is another reason too for alertness at the present time. Modern life, and this applies in varying degrees to all countries, is increasingly controlled by the secular mind. The centralization of the public services and the control of broadcasting, cinemas and press in a few hands provide unrivalled power for permeating the mind of the whole

[1] J. H. Oldham, *Church, Community and State*, p. 25.

community. Where religion has ceased to be influential, or where secular control brushes it aside, wrong assumptions about the nature of man and the purpose of life are easily communicated. There may be no public attack on religion or on the liberties associated with it, but the studied neglect of religion as a fact in community and personal life can be contributory to its slow death. Religion may fade away from sheer desuetude, and the Christian Church may be so by-passed as having no relevance for the common affairs of life that it ceases to be anything more than an interesting survival.

One answer to this modern peril is for Christians, at any rate, to understand their liberty and to use it in all its stimulating diversity—in worship, evangelism, teaching, preaching—for the saving of the community and the healing of the nations.

II SOME PROBLEMS RAISED BY RELIGIOUS LIBERTY

Community Solidarity. It must be admitted that the claim of religious liberty does raise awkward and at times almost insoluble problems for the state, and I have briefly commented on some of them.

Is religious liberty a danger to the homogeneity and solidarity of the state? Does it detract from the loyalties which a state may rightly expect from its members? Is it a divisive rather than a unifying liberty?

In English history the attempt to create a church which would be co-extensive with the nation was partly fostered by the desire for national unity. Tudor, Stuart and Commonwealth men all feared religious liberty, wondering not only how heresy would be dealt with, but how national unity could be preserved, if men were allowed to get their own way in religious matters. What gradually emerged was the realization that state dogmatism and freedom for the

religious man and his community—call it church or sect—
could not exist side by side unless there was a readiness on
every side to recognize each other's rights and liberties.
Andrew Melville, in his famous interview with King James
VI of Scotland, put the point bluntly but clearly to the
king:

> Sir, we will humblie reverence your Majestie alwayes,
> namlie in publick, but sen we have this occasioun to be
> with your Majestie in privat, and the countrey and Kirk
> of Chryst is lyk to wrak, for nocht telling yow the treuthe,
> and giffen of you a faithfull counsall, we maun discharge
> our dewtie thairin, or else be traotors bathe to Chryst
> and yow. And, theirfor, sir, as dyvers tymes befor, sa
> now again I mon tell yow, thair is two kingdomes in
> Scotland. Thair is Chryst Jesus the King, and His King-
> dome the Kirk, whase subject King James the Saxt is,
> and of whase kingdome nocht a king nor a lord nor a
> heid, bot a member. And, sir, when yie war in your
> swaddling-cloutes, Chryst Jesus rang friely in this land in
> spyt of all His enemies.[1]

Lord Acton puts the same point in his *History of Freedom*:

> The feeling of duty and responsibility to God is the
> only arbiter of a Christian's actions. With this no human
> authority can be permitted to interfere. We are bound
> to extend to the utmost, and to guard from every en-
> croachment, the sphere in which we can act in obedience
> to the sole voice of conscience, regardless of any other
> consideration. The Church cannot tolerate any species
> of government in which this right is not recognized. She
> is the irreconcilable enemy of the despotism of the State,
> whatever its name or its forms may be, and through what-
> ever instruments it may be exercised.[2]

Does the modern state in actual practice find religious
liberty and the varieties of religious allegiance it may
engender dangerous? Japan is a recent instance where
state action was used to reorganize the various religious

---

[1] Micklem, *The Theology of Politics*, pp. 87-8.
[2] Acton, op. cit., p. 203.

E

faiths and bring them within the category of registered religions—Shintoism, Buddhism and two sections of the Christian faith, Protestant and Roman Catholic. No doubt the Japanese authorities preferred to deal with three or four large blocks of organized religious life rather than a maze of smaller organizations, and so took the first step towards state control of religion.

Islamic countries, in particular, fear what will happen to their national solidarity if once the groups of varying religious faiths expand and develop. Islam to-day is regarded as a bastion against the spread of materialism and as a uniting force against Russian political penetration. Any threat to the Islamic front from within the nation must therefore be carefully regulated and controlled. The internal rights of the various religious communities with their own laws may be respected, but any expansion of their life is a vital thrust at the heart of Islamic tradition, faith and culture in which the state is embedded. Any Moslem who attempts to change his religion is a traitor both to his faith and his country.

Religious tests for office, preferment or position of leadership in the state are in most modern states an anachronism. It is not so in orthodox Islamic states, nor in states dominated by the Roman Catholic church, and the purist in these matters may even point to the requirement of Protestant belief by the sovereign in order to succeed to the throne of England!

1

Variety rather than uniformity has been the contribution of religious liberty to the modern state. In Britain the mixture of varying types of Christian practice and church order in the life of the state has surely been a strength rather than a drawback. Britain has gained immeasurably from the life of the smaller church fellowships from which have come leaders in local and national government, administrators, educators, trade-union leaders and many generations of people who have quickened and developed our social democratic life. To many of these the Christian religion was the source of their inspiration, and often the local Christian fellowship was the nursing mother of their early training in the meaning of freedom.

Religion frequently finds new power and life in small groups which have a right to expect from the state the same guarantee of liberty and life which the larger societies claim. If mere uniformity in religion be the aim of the state then religious liberty will certainly be in peril. Religion in this respect is a valuable safeguard of general liberties for it is a tutor to the state educating it in the ways of liberty, and exhorting it to expect new and exciting things to emerge from the life of its citizens the more they are truly religious.

Religious freedom, undoubtedly, includes the right to dissent from a requirement of the state. This challenge to a state's solidarity is at its sharpest in a citizen's refusal to give armed service to the state, a conscientious objection held by non-believers, agnostics as well as members of Christian churches. This right of conscientious objection is a high privilege for the individual citizen, and one which a state should meet with understanding and respect. On his part the citizen must realize that his religious freedom is not freedom *from* the responsibilities and duties but freedom *for* duties of citizenship, and that his conscientious objection to certain duties must be accompanied by a zeal in his general devotion as a citizen.

Minorities. Liberty for minorities has nearly always been linked with religious liberty. In some minorities the issue of religious liberty has been the focusing point of all their other liberties, as with the historic Waldensian community in Italy and the Christian communities in Islamic countries. In others religious liberty has been one amongst the general liberties of speech, publication, assembly and freedom from arbitrary interference—the liberties which minorities in the modern state treasure as obvious evidence of their separate existence.

How to deal with minorities has always been a source of trouble and perplexity to modern states. One example of minority settlement is the two hundred years of internal struggle in England which eventually brought contentment to English religious minorities. But could this internal method be honestly recommended as a general course for modern states? Internal settlement has usually meant expulsion, or the uprooting from old attachments, or compulsory absorption. States have varied in their attitudes, and so have minorities in their attitudes to the states in which they live. Europe has had painful examples in both directions in recent years. But there is no avoiding Lord Acton's judgement that the amount of security enjoyed by its minorities is a good test of how far a country is really free.

The most comprehensive international attempt to deal with minority problems was made between 1919-1923 when under the auspices of the League of Nations many minorities treaties were concluded through the League's minorities system. These treaties affected the welfare of thirty million people speaking thirty-six languages, and in every treaty religious liberty was recognized. The League's work on minorities was one of its most successful ventures, and in the realm of religious liberty it was a continuation of the nineteenth-century concern about oppressed minorities which in Britain was aroused by such scandals as the Turkish treatment of Armenian Christians, the treatment of Poles by Czarist Russia, and the Roumanian oppression of the Jews.

An illustration of this period of international action on minorities and religious liberty is contained in the documents which the League approved in May 1937 on the transfer of the Alexandretta district from French Syrian to Turkish administration:

> All inhabitants of the Sanjak shall enjoy full and entire protection for their lives and liberties, without distinction of birth, nationality, language, race or religion.
>
> They shall be entitled to practise freely, both in public and in private, any faith, religion or creed the practice of which is not incompatible with public order and morality.
>
> All citizens of the Sanjak shall be equal before the law, and shall enjoy the same civil and political rights, without distinction of race, language or religion.
>
> No difference of race, religion or language shall cause prejudice to any citizen of the Sanjak in the enjoyment of his civil and political rights, and especially as regards admission to public offices, functions and honours, and the exercise of the various professions and trades.
>
> There shall be absolute freedom of conscience. Citizens shall be entitled to choose any religion they wish. The Sanjak shall have no official religion. No advantage may be granted to any religion or creed to the detriment of any other.[1]

The last article includes the vital phrase " citizens shall be entitled to choose any religion they wish ", an essential element in any safeguard for religious liberty.

What most of the states who between the wars signed minorities treaties wanted, of course, was cultural uniformity rather than religious uniformity, a sense of solidarity within the state to be achieved through a common outlook on racial and economic grounds. Religious differences were to be respected and liberty guaranteed as long as these divergencies did not disrupt the homogeneity of the state. When a critical disruption did take place, as in the Sudetenland German area of Czechoslovakia, it was on grounds of

[1] Quoted Bates, pp. 491f.

69

race rather than religion that the divergence came. During the years of the minorities treaties from 1925 onwards the League held an annual conference of European minorities for discussion of large principles and constructive action rather than the airing of individual grievances. While the League did not solve the minorities question, it did provide for minorities during its years of high prestige a recognized channel of appeal, with an international forum where facts could be made known and free comment heard. That there was little or no religious persecution during this period may be attributed to a growing international conscience about minorities as much as to more favourable internal state conditions.

Something more is called for to-day and that lies in the proposals associated with the Declaration of Human Rights dealt with in the last chapter of this book. This plan would commit all nations to a new declaration of human rights and provide the whole human race with a fresh approach to human freedom. It would have the great merit of removing minority problems from association with national sovereignty and national interest, and place all nations on an equal footing in relation to individual and group freedom.

The Christian Church as an Institution. The Christian Church by reason of its structure raises issues about liberty which are pertinent for the modern state and other institutions within the state. Dogmatic and unbending in its central affirmation that human life finds its meaning and fulfilment in a community of persons, the Church believes that through the revelation of God in Christ such a community is created under the direction of God. A new order breaks into human affairs by divine action; men are adopted as sons of God and are admitted into a life of communion and intercourse with Him. In this sense the Church is not a voluntary association of men for religious purposes which it sometimes appears to be. It is a divine creation where the first things are trust, loyalty, obedience—man's response. to God's invitation.

These beliefs are admittedly awkward ones for administrators, treaty-drafters and politicians whose secular minds frequently fail to find a convenient category into which the Christian Church may be fitted. As a voluntary association it ought to be placed amongst all the other societies whose special interests should be protected. As a cultural force the Christian Church clearly has an important share in general civilization, both as a society committed to educational work and social welfare and humanitarian services.

All these arguments may be used in stating a case for the Christian Church's liberties, but on none of them could the Church finally base its claims which are centred in the great liberty inherent in the life of the Church. Once its divine foundation is recognized the Christian Church is seen to be a state within a state, owning only the Crown Rights of Christ as its ultimate authority.

This claim to liberty by an institution whose courts of law are not in the control of the state is the age-old problem which Christ first stated in His judgement, " Render unto Caesar the things which are Caesar's, and unto God the things which are God's." Right down to our own times the tension between Church and State persists, producing the inevitable clashes, but also sharpening the contentions. Each generation discovers fresh aspects of the main controversy—old paganisms are redressed, and the state periodically steps out to reassert its claims to supremacy.

Everything depends upon the Church being alive at any given moment in history, both to its own position as the Body of Christ, and its place as an institution within an organized state. That is particularly important at the present time when new states are coming into existence where the Christian Church is only a small minority, and where there is no tradition of general freedom respected by both. The older Christendom of the West has a heritage of freedom, largely its own creation, and still lively as a background to state action. No such background can be assumed over large areas of the world to-day, nor can the high claims to religious freedom on the part of the Church be expected to win easy recognition.

As an institution the Christian Church is peculiarly in need of liberty. It is the native air of its community life; and in facing the tensions which its presence in the modern state creates, the Church must be zealous not to lower its conception of liberty. The Church is free because of its divine structure. It is free not on human sufferance, but by reason of its own life under the direction of the Holy Spirit.

The Church must, therefore, take steps wherever necessary to secure reliefs from disabilities imposed by the state, either by changes of law, or by international action. But, frequently, a more far-reaching aim of the Church in a situation where religious liberty is threatened is to understand the causes of the restrictions, and to bring out into the open the theories which prompt them. In this way the Church frees itself of the liability of being dubbed a disloyal organization within the state, and it also strengthens its own inner faith upon which its whole witness to religious freedom depends. As an institution the Church will in many modern states be bound to accept certain working restrictions under protest. This amount of compromise is justified as long as the Church regularly reminds itself and the state of the full meaning of the liberty in the Christian Gospel, and is prepared to suffer if need be, when its minimum rights and liberties are disregarded.

The Place of Missions. For Christianity religious liberty must mean freedom to preach and persuade—the basis of the missionary enterprise which is the life-blood of the

Christian faith. Any threat to the freedom of missions, or the liberties of individual missionaries, is a denial of religious liberty in the Christian interpretation of it. This raises issues for the state in which missions are carried on, and also for the religions already present in the land.

Christianity's missionary calling rises naturally through the person and work of Christ. Missions are not a human addendum to the Christian religion, but are essential to its whole life as a universal religion and to the Church as a supra-national fellowship. This means that missions prove a unique testing-ground on nearly all matters connected with religious liberty.

It is an essential demand of the Christian Church that it shall be allowed to carry on missions, a claim maintained from its early days and prosecuted with remarkable vigour in modern times. There are still countries, however, which forbid Christian missions to enter, such as Tibet, Afghanistan and Saudi Arabia; and Moslem lands where they work under acute restrictions which deny liberty of action. But with these exceptions Christian missions have secured their freedom by general consent in most countries, purchased originally through the sturdy witness of early pioneers. Religious liberty for missions and missionaries means liberty to come and go, liberty to move about unhindered and within a given territory, liberty to preach, persuade, teach and distribute the Scriptures, with due respect to public order and the sovereignty of the state.

The missionary needs freedom, too, to interpret another aspect of his mission—the supra-nationalism of the Gospel of which he is the representative in a unique way. He in his own person communicates the universality of the Christian religion, and while remaining a loyal citizen of his own country, witnesses by his presence to the Kingdom which he believes is above all kingdoms.

These claims may easily be misconstrued, and the missionary dubbed as a foreign agent trying to secure a foothold for his own country and its policies. There were instances amongst German missionaries in the second world war where charges of this kind seemed proved, but most missionaries by their personal integrity and loyalty to their vocation have shown their respect for the freedom granted them in foreign countries. But it cannot be denied that the present pattern of dogmatic nationalism is bound to be suspicious of the foreign missionary and his motives in a manner which was not present during the nineteenth century outreach of foreign missions. Then freedom of missions frequently had the protection of the European powers which were dominant in Africa, India and the East, and while no mission officially claimed protection, consuls and diplomatic representatives were, at least, aware of their presence and gave advice in emergencies. Modern nationalist governments cannot be expected to grant privileges of freedom on grounds of nationality alone. Missions must claim their freedom on the highest grounds of their origin and purpose, and must divest themselves of any trait of foreignness in their methods.

This is where the growth of the Church is an exceedingly important contributory factor to missionary freedom. The modern missionary goes increasingly to serve in and through the church of the land of his adoption, taking his directions for service from that church. His freedom is linked with the freedom of the church which must preserve, in negotiations with the state, the right to use men and women of other nationalities in its service. This may well be a peril for a young church trying to be loyal to a national pattern, and it may easily be led to dispense with foreign missionaries (as the Japanese church agreed to do at the behest of the state in 1940) and thus lose its ecumenical character.

2

It may be useful to add a note here on the status of missions under some of the principal colonial governments. Foreign missionaries in British Africa are regarded as immigrants and come under the laws which apply to them. Legally they are liable to pay deposits on entry, but in the case of established missions holding property this is usually waived. The general policy in British colonial territories is that of tolerance, or strict neutrality, towards varying religious beliefs, although in areas of fanatical Moslem influence Christian missions are restricted and in some cases (Somaliland and several Indian states) are not admitted. British policy is to use missions positively in the service of the people, subsidizing their work in education, medicine and social welfare, but still maintaining the policy of toleration towards religious belief.

The French attitude to missions has been affected by the relations of Church and State in France and the lay position of the state which has resulted in a special body of legal regulations which carefully define the limits within which missions may carry on their activities. French anxiety to assimilate the inhabitants of colonial territories and to encourage the assumption of French citizenship and culture tend to make administrations suspicious of non-French religious missions, an attitude which has been allayed by loyal co-operation on the part of missions since the difficult periods of the nineteenth century. The right to teach is controlled by local administrators who may grant requests for schools provided that teaching is in French except in the case of simple catechumen schools.

In the Belgian Congo—one of the great areas of Christian expansion—missions work under a charter which states that the Governor General shall protect and favour without distinction of nationality and cult. In general, however, there is an undeniable leaning towards favouring Roman Catholic missions. In the Congo land concessions, up to 1937, 118,000 acres were granted to 50 Roman Catholic missions and about 5,000 to 31 Protestant ones, and in subsidies as much as 34,000,000 francs have been paid in one year to Roman Catholic missions and only 77,000 francs to Protestant ones. About 16,000,000 francs are paid over every year to subsidize Roman Catholic schools for education work, but nothing to Protestant ones although there are a quarter of a million children in Protestant schools compared with 480,000 in Roman Catholic schools.

One of the accusations against missions in Portuguese colonial areas is that they tend to "denationalize" the people and are suspected of carrying on an underhand campaign against national sovereignty by, for instance, teaching in the vernacular instead of in Portuguese. Most of these charges when examined are groundless because evangelical missions in Portuguese areas have been scrupulous in their attempts to train up good Portuguese Christian citizens, and the success of Protestant pupils in public examinations is evidence of their loyalty as citizens. Religious liberty in these areas is threatened by the double influence of nationalism and a dominant religion, Roman Catholicism, while in the French Empire it is the state with its strict legal requirements which may hinder the free growth of religious bodies.

III   YOUNGER CHRISTENDOM

Nothing is more important to the life and well-being of the younger Christendom which has come into existence during the last 150 years than religious liberty.

In one sense the very existence of these younger churches in countries like India, China, Africa and Japan is due to the liberty of preaching and persuasion exercised by the churches of Europe and America inspired by the evangelical passions roused in the nineteenth century. Liberty then was a watchword which infected religious as well as political and economic movements. Under the compulsion of a personal urge men and women gave themselves to the task of taking the Gospel to other countries at sacrifices which daunted few of them, and the results are seen in the living Christian fellowships to-day.

A sharply defined and rigidly held theology was the basis of the nineteenth-century expansion of the Christian faith, and that theology also implied freedom of expression and freedom of movement for its believers, a belief which carried William Carey to India in spite of the prohibitions of the East India Company. To be confined even in one place was an irritation for such men as Williams in the South Seas and Livingstone in Africa. They claimed the liberty of the Gospel to cross the oceans and the continents to display the truth of the Christian revelation as one for the whole world. Governments and states, although they gave little active support—such as Spain and Portugal provided during a previous missionary expansion—did nothing effective to check this spontaneous growth. Many of them welcomed missions for what civilized values might accrue from their progress, but in no country was the Christian Church favoured and recognized as it had been in the West. No Constantine has appeared amongst the rulers of the East to throw a mantle of recognition over the invading faith. On some Pacific islands the ruling houses by their conversion in the early nineteenth century did precipitate small " mass movements " to the new faith amongst their subjects, but in the thickly populated East no ruler has been ready to stamp the Christian faith with his personal and official approval. Strongly entrenched ancient religions intermixed with the social life of the country faced the new faith in the old civilizations, especially in India. Those religions, often depicted by early missionaries as moribund if not dead, were themselves stirred into fresh life by Christianity's aggressiveness, with the result that Christianity, in the main, has had to work and fight hard for its victories with often unrewarded zeal for long stretches of time.

The Christian churches which to-day constitute the younger Christendom are the fruits, humanly speaking, of much lonely faithfulness and unheralded devotion on the part of quite ordinary men and women from Europe and America. Famous pioneers played their part and performed many miracles, but the true founders of the younger churches and builders of their early liberties are the uncelebrated missionaries who possessed a working confidence that the Gospel they preached could become indigenous in the soil and culture of other countries than their own. This is not to overlook or discount in any way the work of Indian, Chinese and Japanese Christians in the early days of Christian missionary work—they share this glory; that the Gospel came to them through the medium of " foreigners " is evidence of the genius of the faith to grow in fresh soil once it is given liberty to take root.

1

In facing its religious liberty problems younger Christendom knows that in every land it is mainly a minority group. Even in China and India the number of Christians is extremely small in proportion to the vast populations, a position which confronts organized Christianity with delicate issues of prestige and protection. Should it regard itself merely (as in most Islamic countries) as a registered cult alongside other religious cults, or seek special privileges in worship, education and propaganda? Should it be content with its own life as a comparatively small community, or be alert and restless in its evangelism and propaganda? How must it regard a state which is identified with a particular religion, or one which is definitely anti-religious, or one which unites nationalism and secularism?

It should be obvious that no church in the younger Christendom can claim special privileges which may be denied to other religions. Christianity does not ask for state establishment or official favours, but for liberty. In countries where, however, British power has a paramountcy there may be links between the state and the church for particular purposes, such as education, a situation existing mainly in Africa and other British colonial territories. In India, in the past, Christianity undoubtedly had official favours shown to it but no one expects or even desires this kind of favour in the future. Christianity will flourish in the new India if it is allowed to present the truth unhindered and without patronage.

There is, however, a danger to the life of younger Christendom which only a spacious and regularly renewed conception of religious liberty can avoid. The attitude to religion in the past of the lay, or secular, state is to register religious communities communally (as in India), or to confer official recognition on a number of religions (as in Iran), a method ensuring administrative efficiency by practically condemning the recognized religion to a walled existence unless it is wise and alert about its liberties. Christianity has an important contribution to make here for the sake of all religions. It alone has a theological and doctrinal basis defined sharply enough to withstand state pressure—not a new unknown terror in the history of the Christian faith. If the East does not repeat the experiences of the West, and the whole climate of state and religion are infinitely removed from anything Europe knows, yet there is a certain basis of action in regard to liberty that Christianity has learned, and which may guide a new and growing Christendom.

It should be assumed that the state has a goodwill to all its citizens until the contrary is proved. Christianity has everything to gain by acting on this assumption if it is alert enough at the same time to be watchful of state action. While the younger Christendom must inevitably come to terms with the state, as did the older Christendom, it should approach this chastening and character-forming adventure in the knowledge that it has a ministry to the rising national states in the East which issues naturally from its belief in liberty. It has something both to say and do in friendship to the state which will make the Christian Church a priceless asset to the national life, and the Christian man, with his citizenship laid up in heaven, also a citizen of the first quality here on earth.

Take, for example, India and her communal question which dominates her political, religious and cultural life. It is not too much to claim that Indian Christians are the only Indians with an " all India " outlook free from the bonds of communal nationalism. An experienced observer of the India scene writes:

It is notable that for the Christians " India " is their natural and spontaneous outlook. The strength of the Christian position and its real power is in its non-communal outlook, its all-Indian outlook, if you like. This has been observed and envied by others. There is among the Christians, with all their faults, that something which India needs now—a personal sense of liberation and a conscious appreciation of religious liberty. This quality of the Christian character and outlook needs no legal sanctions. The strength of the Christian position is the quality of the contribution the Christian can make to the new India. Many instances could be given of the way this works out in Indian public life, and if the relations between Hindus and Moslems continue to deteriorate, this will become more and more noticeable. . . . Only if Christians take their stand on this quality of the service which they can render will they be appreciated. India

80

must solve her own problem of religious liberty and face the period—long or short—of considerable trial and error before it finds its feet in the new world now opening before it.[1]

India is now two nations,[2] " with no common culture, no universally recognized pattern of life, no generally accepted religious sanctions ".[3] Christianity's constructive contribution to India's national life lies in its universal sense which sees the wholeness of India's life and aspirations, and sets out to mould and unify diverse opposites. It took a thousand years to accomplish that task in the older Christendom. How long in the younger?

I once heard an Indian remark that the only place where Hindu and Moslem young men met in a friendly way in his district was in the Christian college. There the transforming process of making real Indians was at work, liberating a new nationalism neither caste nor communal bound, but truly Indian in its horizons. Christian freedom has this gift to offer to the nations of a younger Christendom performing a similar purification to the new nations as it did for the old.

2

There are, however, radically different elements in the struggle for religious liberty in the new Christendom as compared with the old. Christianity's slow evolution to toleration in the West was almost a domestic affair. There was internally no other religion to challenge its position, and the state, while adamant in its own defence, was also ardent for the Christian religion and favoured no other. How different is the religious climate in which the younger Christendom is growing up! With no favours, and intense opposition in many countries, Christianity can only expect

---

[1] Quoted *C.M.S. News Letter*, No. 76, November 1946.
[2] Pakistan being predominantly Moslem.
[3] Quoted *C.M.S. News Letter*, No. 76, November 1946.

F

liberty for itself by demanding it for all. It should press in India for a general declaration of religious liberty, supported by all religions and in particular by the two great faiths— Hindu and Moslem.

Mr. Nehru has already declared himself on the general question of religious liberty in India in an interview:

> Although our ultimate aim is a secular state not to be identified with any particular religion, freedom of conscience and the recognition of the religious rights of all citizens must be the starting-point. Indian Christians are part and parcel of the Indian people. Their traditions go back 1,500 years and more, and they form one of the many enriching elements in the country's cultural and spiritual life. . . .[1]

All this confirms the view that the right approach is to assume the goodwill of the state to all its citizens, unless the contrary is proved, and in all cases to understand the underlying reasons for state action, and to remove misunderstandings. What the younger Christendom asks in terms of religious liberty are the universal liberties of freedom of worship, freedom to persuade, to teach, to propagate, to print. This involves the right to change one's religion and belief without any diminution of civil rights, in fact, to be a citizen without the handicap of prejudice due to religious profession. Most of this sounds axiomatic to those brought up in the liberal atmosphere of the Western world, but little of it is natural and inevitable in the East. Rights of this kind are foreign to the social and cultural make-up of Islamic countries and of Hindu India where the solidarity of the social structure is bound up with religious observances, so that anyone changing his allegiance at once threatens anarchy. It is this fear, quite as much as any religious conviction, which governs the attitude of many Eastern states towards Christianity and its mission-

[1] Reported *Ecumenical Press Service*, No. 29, August 1946.

ary purpose. Will freedom to persuade, teach and propagate be a menace to the state's foundations? Will an otherwise stable situation in which everyone has his regulated position be rendered unstable?

These questions are very potent ones in some countries where the younger Christendom has taken root, and where it may appear to be a cause of unrest and dissidence. Claims to religious liberty are consequently affected by social and political apprehensions as much as by religious bigotry. Christianity's chief mission for liberty in such circumstances is to press the claims of religious liberty for all citizens irrespective of creed, a service which is of supreme value for the welfare of the state.

It is important for Western Christendom to realize that the younger Christendom is growing up in countries still immature politically, and with few guarantees of liberty as they are regarded in the West. This is at once an opportunity and a danger for Christianity. Its adaptiveness and cohesive power, so brilliantly displayed in the West, are provided with fresh fields of conquest, but the strong tides of nationalism have to be reckoned with. Nationalism takes varied forms. In India it is saturated with religious sanctions but with a strongly communist-agnostic tinge; in China, outwardly tolerant but with lay secularism in administrative control; in Japan, a chastened nationalism still under occupational control; Indonesia and Burma, a nascent national life in which minorities must look to their rights and liberties; in Turkey, a secular nationalism impatient altogether with religion; in Egypt and the Arab countries, the Islamic " church-state " pattern, well equipped and alert to maintain its integrity.

In all these seething situations full religious liberty is yet to be achieved. It cannot, to say the least, be taken for granted that the new nations now rising in the East will jump with alacrity into practising all the liberties which mature nations have taken long years to secure. Religious liberty in particular is the fruit of mature political and religious experience. In history it is really the last of human liberties, and it may be that its possession will be secured in the East only through some of the agony which accompanied its birth in the West. If so, the younger Christendom has now a strategic part to play in the process of education. It must be a tutor to the new states, as an older Christendom was tutor to the Western world, showing them that the well-being of states varies directly with the amount of liberty granted to its citizens both in personal and social affairs. It must also go on to show that in a state where several religious communities are living side by side, harmony and happiness for them and the state are only possible when toleration is both granted and guaranteed. To preserve national unity in spite of religious differences is only possible under toleration—a lesson which may well be one of the younger Christendom's most significant contributions to the world of new nations.

IV   TO PRACTISE AND TO PROPAGATE

" It stands to reason ", said Mr. Nehru when asked about Indian Christians' freedom not only to practise but to propagate their religion, " that any faith whose roots are strong and healthy should spread; and to interfere with that right to spread seems to me to be a blow at the roots themselves. . . . In a country with so many creeds as India we must learn to be tolerant. For the sake of harmony we shall have to respect the religious convictions of all, irrespective of numbers and influence. Unless a given faith proves a menace to public order, or its teachers attempt to thrust it down the unwilling throats of men of other persuasions, there can be no justification for measures which deprive any community of its rights."[1]

[1] Reported interview, *Ecumenical Press Service*, No. 79, August 1946.

Similarly Mr. Jinnah on July 13, 1947, at a press conference, " gave an ample unqualified assurance to the
minorities that there would be adequate safeguards for
their religion, property, culture and freedom of worship,
but minorities must remain loyal to their own state and owe
it true allegiance. This principle applied to the minorities
of both Dominions."[1]

Mr. Nehru's statement sets out at any rate one reason for
the full freedom of any religion to propagate itself—that it
is a rational act on the part of any healthy organism. As
far as Christianity is concerned it is always a test of its
health and vitality to see how vigorously it is propagating
itself. The structure of the Christian religion and its basic
doctrines force Christianity into missionary methods, and
anyone who misguidedly thinks it is active in propaganda
on the ground of petty busyness or uninformed interference
is seriously misjudging the grounds for Christianity's existence. I need not go into these reasons again as they have
been treated in other sections of this book, except to say
that liberty to practise and propagate, or to persuade men
to become Christians is a crucial issue right at the heart of
the meaning of religious liberty for Christianity.

In discussing the right to persuade men to change their
religious allegiance, or the Christian obligation to witness
to others, we pass out of the realm of legal right into that
of religious duty. Christian practice carries with it the duty
of witness to others—it cannot be called Christian without
it, and the danger that threatens any Christian community
which omits its duty of witnessing is poignantly illustrated
in Christian history. Christianity propagates or it perishes.
States may guarantee religious freedom, and there may be
an amplitude of facilities for religious expression and discussion, but the Christian man does not finally base his
claim to propagate his faith on any legal right. In this

[1] Reported *Manchester Guardian*, July 14, 1947.

matter he is under obedience. He is not so much claiming a legal right as obeying a spiritual duty to God.

All this sounds practicable enough in a British atmosphere, but the Christian faith finds itself set in a number of varied national atmospheres some of which are often inimical to Christian witness. In the Near East and Asia the tides of nationalism flowing strongly between the two world wars have increased in strength, and new nations are now taking shape and independence, as in Egypt, India, Burma and Indonesia. Nationalism claims the high allegiance of the most vigorous and enlightened groups in all these lands, and the fact of the state (whether it be called " planned ", " welfare " or " totalitarian ") is paramount.

It used to be a customary comment, for instance, before the second world war that the European liberal tradition was playing an important part in liberalizing the ancient ways of Islamic lands, and there was much evidence to support the view. But observers in the Near East now report a rehardening of the traditional Islamic pattern, and consequently an increasing sensitiveness to any form of religious propaganda contrary to Islam. Heavy blows and almost complete disaster have been suffered by the Western liberal tradition—with which Christianity is historically associated—and they have not gone unnoticed by the younger generations of Asia's new countries. There has been a turning inwards on the old faiths and a resurgence of interest in them as the fortress of national traditions and the centre of national hopes and aspirations. Observers in India see this in a revived interest in Hinduism and a re-kindled loyalty in the younger generation to its observances. This movement is even more noticeable in Islam where, for example, in Egypt there is a renewed fervour for the " church-state " of Islam under pressure of a dogmatic nationalism.

1

It is not easy for anyone brought up in the Western conception of individual right and freedom to conceive of a situation, as in Egypt, where only Moslems have full rights and non-Moslems have only limited rights. That is the kernel of the religious freedom situation in Egypt and in other Islamic lands. Religious change is not recognized; in fact, it is thought inconceivable that a Moslem should change his faith, and any attempt to persuade him to do so is an affront at both national and religious solidarity.

In the Egyptian Constitution (formulated in 1923) are to be found all the phrases which satisfy the mind and the emotions of a Westerner—personal liberty, liberty of conscience, liberty of opinion and freedom of education. But article 149 is the ruling declaration—" Islam is the religion of the State ". This means in practice that the government defends Islam against any other religion, and that in making appointments to public offices preference is given to Moslems which in practice compels large numbers of Coptic Christians each year to become nominal Moslems for economic reasons.

Under the Montreux Capitulations of 1937, which govern the present position of religious bodies in Egypt, freedom of worship is assured, but difficulties frequently occur when permits are sought for the erection of new churches, and as schools and offices open on Sundays this has a serious effect on the spiritual life of the Christian community. A further disability is the community court. There are fifteen of these courts in Egypt, each with its own special jurisdiction and codes designed to meet the needs of the various religious communities. Moslems object to their presence, and the community frequently finds that the court is not fully competent to deal with all cases. For example, when the two parties to a suit belong to different Christian churches the case must be tried by a Sharia (Moslem) court which is held competent in all circumstances—a galling fact for anyone who is trying to be a good Egyptian and a good Christian at the same time.

It is precisely this latter fact which legally is an impossibility because in Egypt there is no legal recognition of conversion to Christianity. Born a Moslem you remain one and are subject to Sharia law, and even though you may call yourself by another name your personal status in the eyes of Moslem law remains unchanged. It ought, therefore, to be possible to retain all the privileges of your Moslem birth such as inheritance of property, but, as more than one case has shown, the Sharia court denies even this right to the " pervert ". In the case of a Moslem woman of mature years becoming a Christian she is handed over according to the Sharia law to the guardianship of her nearest Moslem relatives even though she has borne a child to her Christian husband. So anyone who is led to become a Christian finds himself in a morass of predicaments and the edge of Christian evangelism is effectively blunted.

Every few years in Egypt a wave of anti-missionary feeling sweeps up, frequently inflamed by disgruntled elements but nearly always providing an illustration of the tension which exists. The last occasion—widely noted at the time—was in 1932, and the circumstances, already public,[1] are worth recalling. In November 1928 a Moslem girl, educated at a mission school, expressed her desire to become a Christian and after instruction was baptized. Her father was dead and her mother raised no objections. Four years later she was married to a Christian teacher in the presence of her mother and two sisters. In March 1933 the mother began to show signs of hostility, maintaining that the young man had deceived her by pretending that he was a Moslem. The girl wavered and said she wished to return

[1] *International Review of Missions*, October 1933, p. 530.

to Islam, but though this was later repudiated the Sharia court held that she was a Moslem and that her marriage was null and void. Her grandfather was persuaded to claim guardianship, but the court of the Protestant community judged that the marriage was in order and that the girl was in the guardianship of her husband. So the case had to be referred to a special court in the Ministry of Justice, and eventually the husband and wife were happily reunited.

While this case was being discussed another " incident " originating in the same mission school precipitated a crisis. A pupil was deliberately rude and insubordinate, and a missionary member of the staff took a cane and hit the girl, who immediately lodged a complaint with the police that she had been beaten because she refused to embrace Christianity. Feeling in Port Said ran high, the government demanded that all Moslem children should be handed over to their parents and guardians, and voted £E70,000 for the erection of orphanages for Moslem children. The girl also showed the police letters from missionary friends, some of which contained over-persuasive expressions of Christian belief unsuitable for a Moslem girl of fifteen.

These facts provided enough fuel for a violent campaign against missions and their evangelistic plans. Newspapers conducted " enquiries " into missionary work and " exposed " their objectives and methods. They were described as imperialistic in design and tools of foreign powers having as their aim the destruction of Islam. Their school books, literature and teaching were said to degrade Islam and disparage the prophet and his book, and their social and philanthropic activities were only cloaks for their evangelistic aims. Sickness, ignorance and poverty were said to be exploited in order to persuade the weak and defenceless to become Christians. Where persuasion failed compulsion was used in order to secure attendance at Christian prayers and instruction in mission hospitals and institutions, and—worst of all—young children were forced to listen to Bible teaching, to pray Christian prayers, and were secretly baptized. It was even stated that missionaries used immoral and vicious methods in order to achieve their vile purposes with young people. The campaign, however, overshot its mark even in Egyptian eyes, when it was stated that a prominent Moslem, once a patient in a missionary hospital, had been offered £E50 a month if he would become a Christian!

Out of this grew a further agitation that the government should draft a law curtailing evangelistic work among Moslems, and in 1940 the King signed an order for submission to parliament of a law which, if passed, would have done this. Although it was not proceeded with, it is not impossible to conceive circumstances in Egypt demanding its revival. In the Christian view much of the tension would be removed if Egypt would allow the legal recognition of conversion to Christianity as in the Western Sudan, Palestine, Iraq and the Lebanon—a method which removes contentious and irritating personal disabilities as in the laws of inheritance and in the personal rights of women converts. To do this, however, means a revolution in public opinion even more than a legal revolution in a land like Egypt. No Moslem is really convinced that anyone changes from Islam to another faith by his own free will. There must, he believes, be some other motive, some pressure or undue persuasion at work to bring about this unthinkable act. While that attitude remains, freedom to persuade—even if recognized legally—will be suspected, a situation which compels all Christian agencies rigorously to examine their motives as well as their methods.

There is a marked hardening of Islamic sentiment in Egypt, with the government lending much official support in advancing the prestige of Islam. That has resulted in an increasing number of restrictive measures designed to limit the sphere of missionary activity. Some of these measures (as in the 1940 bill) have failed to become law because the distinction between Moslem and non-Moslem propaganda was not clear. But there was little doubt that the framers of the particular bill had Christian institutions in mind.

I have burrowed through a stack of correspondence which has accumulated in Britain during the last twenty years on questions of religious freedom in Egypt. I am not at liberty to make quotations from it, but I can record the feeling of suffocation and impotence which arose as I read of the small Christian communities struggling in an Islamic atmosphere to be true to their calling as Christians. Legalities, definitions and explanations abounded in the correspondence, and one sensed the meticulous anxiety of Christian groups not to give cause for accusation as disruptors of the public peace or as agents for attack on Islam. Their future is a hard and anxious one.

2

Turkey is an illustration of how almost the exact opposite of the Egyptian situation may also frustrate freedom. In Turkey the progressives have created a state once described as a " militant race-conscious nationalism ". It has swung away violently from the dominance of Islam although the old religion still has social influence. Turkey is a secular state, and while there is freedom of thought and worship, and liberty to change one's religion without any legal procedure for registration, " evangelism is disapproved and medical and educational institutions are restrained from doing anything either formally and publicly or quietly and privately which can be supposed to influence the minds of those whom they directly benefit towards a change of religion ".[1] For instance the only non-Moslem clergyman

[1] Madras Reports, Vol. VI, p. 117.

who may appear outside his place of worship in official clerical robes is the spiritual head of the community. Theoretically religious instruction may be given by one person to any other who is over eighteen years of age, provided the relationship between them is not officially that of teacher to pupil or doctor to patient. Congregations have to provide a time-table of their services, and all properties of Christian churches are under a branch of the Ministry of the Interior who accepts (by competitive examination) one secular trustee as responsible for the properties of a particular congregation. There is nothing to prevent a Moslem being appointed trustee of a Christian congregation. Unnotified religious gatherings of five or more people are theoretically illegal, and within the past five years a group of sixteen Seventh Day Adventists meeting for worship in a private house in an Istanbul suburb were arrested and taken to a police station where they had to promise to discontinue their meetings. It is important to add that difficulties experienced by Christian communities in Turkey are probably not so severe as those which the Moslems suffer, for in their case determination to preserve the secular character of the state is sharpened by the fear of internal disorder centred in the old religion.

Iran follows Turkey in its general bent towards national homogeneity and national strength, with less drastic measures than in Turkey, and a much more favourable attitude. All members of the Cabinet and other high officials, however, must be Moslems. The four recognized religions—Islam, Zoroastrianism, Christianity and Judaism may worship, propagate, publish their literature, but only Moslems are able to use the radio for religious purposes. Christianity, however, enjoys a large amount of freedom for evangelistic purposes, and hundreds of Moslems and non-Christians have been converted to Christianity, and to-day it is possible to travel everywhere to sell literature, distribute Bibles, and even to lecture on Christianity in government schools. While the legal status of converts from Islam is uncertain an adult Christian when marrying may register as a Christian, and converts are not separated from their own people as is often the case in other Moslem lands. Politics rather than a fanatical religion govern the possibility of fuller religious freedom in Iran. Before the Allied armies occupation, during the war, Reza Shah's influence stimulated anti-freedom movements. Since then the activities of Russia in the North have led those who fear any weakening of the Islamic barrier to Communism to be unfriendly to Christianity. It is in this uncertain atmosphere, without any strong guarantees by the state for their essential liberties, that religious communities have to live. Christianity makes the most use it can of its present freedoms which apart from the compulsory closing of missionary schools are not ungenerous, but how long will they last, and what assurance is there of a progressive policy and religious liberty on the part of the state?

Leaving the Near East we go to the small Indian state of Patna for an extreme example of legislation designed to prevent a change of religion. Situated in the Central Provinces, Patna is a state of some 2,400 square miles with a population of 278,000, and under its Freedom of Religion Act (1942) a person desiring to become a convert to another religion must present himself in person to the Registrar and sign a written statement on oath and pay a fee of one rupee. He may be given a copy of the entry in the Register of Conversions on a payment of a further four annas. In the case of husband and wife wishing to change their religion the Registrar is authorized to examine them to discover whether they are acting under undue influence—and to disallow the application if he thinks so! Here are all the elements of an effective barrier against change in a small peasant state. The long process of registering his conversion plus the payment of one rupee (a small fortune for an Indian peasant), and the certainty of an unfavourable inquisition will prove almost insuperable obstacles to religious change.

One section of the Patna Act is open to the greatest objection of all. It deals with the custody of children when parents become converts. If the children are minors then the father's kinsmen are to have the custody of them, and if the only surviving parent be the mother and she is converted, and if it is considered proper in the public interests to take the child from her, then he may be kept in a recognized orphanage until he is of age.

In the Raigarh and Udaipur States there are similar acts usually promulgated to ensure that subjects shall not be exploited by unscrupulous persons. In Udaipur no lay preachers are permitted to enter the state, but recognized clergymen may enter on giving information to the police about their plans and limiting their stay to forty-eight hours. They must not conduct any religious propaganda outside the membership of their own churches.[1]

These are admittedly extreme examples, and alongside them must be placed the considered statements of Mr. Nehru, the favourable debates on freedom in the Constituent Assembly and such actions as that of Mr. Azad, the President of Congress, who after an attack on a Methodist church building in Calcutta went to present his regrets to the minister and expressed the opinion " that in the India of the future the places of worship of every community would be sacred to members of every other community ".[2]

V   LIBERTY TO TEACH

The state is the greatest educator in the modern world.

[1] *National Christian Council Review*, March 1946, p. 80.
[2] ibid., April 1946, p. 93.

That statement needs modification, but in the main it is true.

Even before the modern " welfare state " developed its present activities of direction and control in education the theories behind the absolutist state were clear to anyone who looked for them. As far back as Plato the state was never happy about rivals to its authority. Then it was the family, and now the Church is added. The belief that the child is the property of the state and can therefore be moulded in its own image sounds Hitlerian, but it was a doctrine full-blown during the French Revolution.

Control education, control the teachers, control the children—these are no new discoveries of the 1940's, but are implicit in the doctrine of the modern state. Once the place of the state is admitted then the citizen must prepare himself to see it wax and develop, and it is certain to be at its liveliest in the field of education.

Having raised the danger signals about the state the Christian man, of all men, must go on to recognize that the state is of divine origin. Only when it becomes an end in itself, glorifying its own existence and deifying its character does it become dangerous to liberty. To be peevish and suspicious about state action in education is to disregard the state's proper function in seeing that every child has the opportunity and the training which will fit it best for life. This mission cannot entirely be fulfilled by parents alone in the modern world, nor with the co-operation of the Church only. There obviously must be co-operation between all three—parents, state and church. It may easily be an unequal partnership dominated by the state with all the modern devices of propaganda and control, but it can also be a working partnership in which liberty is desired and rights are respected.

Britain is trying to work an educational partnership of

this kind. The state has rightly taken the lead in refashioning the educational system, but it has not trampled on the liberties of the Church, or on the freedom of any religious group to maintain schools and to teach, provided the institutions are up to a required standard and the choices of parents are respected. And in its own schools the state has insisted on religious education being given from which any parent has the right to withdraw his child if he so wishes.

This finely balanced partnership is a typically British achievement which naturally does not meet with universal approval either from the churches, or from those who believe in the thorough secularization of education. But it is important from the point of view of religious liberty that the state recognizes the religious basis of education and is prepared to assist religious organizations without controlling them or prescribing the content of their teaching. This is happening in a land where Christianity is the dominant religion, and where there is an assumption that the state itself has a Christian character, but the freedom in question is undoubtedly one for all religions.

British methods can hardly be transplanted into other political settings. The United States of America, for instance, has a sharp distinction between church and state with a prohibition of sectarian instruction in the public schools. Individual states may vary in permission to use the Bible in schools, while in a number of communities the system of a " released time " operates whereby pupils are allowed to go for certain periods to receive denominational instruction, normally off the school premises. In 1940 nearly five hundred educational authorities (one in eight throughout the U.S.A.) had the " released time " method covering a million pupils, but it is estimated that fifteen million American children had no religious instruction whatever by means of the public schools.

This " missing factor " of religion in American education is deplored by many educationists, who, while upholding the separation of church and state, believe that the weight of state influence is too one-sided, and even subsidizes that which is pagan and irreligious. To put the criticism in the words of Dean Weigle of Yale Divinity School, " for the state not to include in its educational programme a definite recognition of the place and value of religion in human life is to convey to children, with all the prestige and authority of the school maintained by the state, the suggestion that religion has no real place and value ".[1] It has had, however, some good effects. American churches are probably better organized to give systematic religious education than most groups of Christian churches, and the number and variety of private schools of religious foundation is a testimony to the awareness by American Christians of their problem. America's method has been a potent example for the rising nations of the world. It is clear-cut, decisive and simplified for statesmen and administrators, and it is admittedly one solution of the baffling problems raised by denominational differences.

1

China has chosen a similar method in constructing her public system of education. There is no recognition of private elementary schools which include religious instruction, but at the higher grade and middle schools and colleges there are courses in religion and voluntary religious exercises. At the university grade the thirteen Christian universities and colleges are lively and efficient examples of institutions imbued with Christian principles and practice. France's secularism in public education is combined with complete freedom in instruction and worship in private

[1] Quoted Bates, p. 340.

schools, and in Germany (before the Nazis) public assistance was given to secular and denominational schools alike. Norway and Sweden require compulsory religious instruction in all schools with exemption for pupils whose parents are not members of the state church. Belgium requires religious instruction in all public elementary schools—usually Roman Catholic—but with exemption clauses, and in the Netherlands, where more than half the elementary schools are denominational, there is public support for confessional schools with a great deal of internal freedom in management.

Asked, in the interview already mentioned, about Christian schools and their future in India, Mr. Nehru replied, " Yes, I think they will continue. Educational institutions of various kinds will survive. It is possible to classify the many schools and colleges set up and maintained by Christians with such institutions."[1] Mr. Nehru conceives a secular state responsible for, and controlling, education as part of its planned economy, and that day plainly lies ahead in India. The Christian Church which has done so much magnificent pioneer work in education in India must learn to accommodate itself to the new situation. A country like India with such vast and enlarged problems of education, with three-fifths of the world's illiterates amongst her population, most of them living in hundreds of thousands of small villages, cannot be tackled educationally by the unrelated efforts of private agencies. We must have sympathy with the state in its endeavour to make a plan. The state cannot propagate one religion, and as it finds it impossible to get an agreed policy amongst the religious denominations, the only education it can enforce and make universal is a secular one. Writing about the new educational policy of the independent Travancore State, Mr. Srinivasa Sastri says:

[1] *Ecumenical Press Service*, August 1946.

The Government of Travancore, with the object of introducing order, justice and progress in the system of primary education, proposes to take it over as a state concern, make it free and compulsory, raise the necessary buildings, appoint competent staffs and find all the other equipment which the present day may require. All communities and religions are made welcome to these new institutions.

No religion will be taught to the pupils as an integral part of the curriculum. If any section of parents wish to teach their religion to their children they may do it at their own cost, but it must be out of school hours, and under necessary restriction to avoid confusion and clash. That is as far as the modern state can go in the direction of affording facilities for religious instruction.[1]

While this new situation will sharpen the Christian community's responsibility for its own children in the schools it chooses to maintain, it will also drive it to find a place in the national systems of Indian education, through the use of hostels, places of residence, chapels, university houses and, above all, by training Christian teachers to take their share in the public schemes. India has been set a high standard of education by Christian institutions, with complete academic freedom as well as definite Christian instruction. Only in a tolerant atmosphere can such academic freedom be guarded, and there are signs in India that even that may be threatened.

An instance of threats both to academic and religious freedom is contained in the action of Bombay University in 1942 and 1944 in which Sophia College (a Roman Catholic institution) was recommended for disaffiliation because two of its Parsee girl students had been received into the Roman church. In August 1943 the Senate carried a resolution affirming " the fundamental policy of the University which is not to permit in any educational institution conducted by

[1] *National Christian Council Review*, October 1946, p. 289.

or affiliated to it, any activity which has for its object the conversion of students from one religion to another ".[1] It was immediately seen, by those not blinded by religious prejudice, that here was a threat to academic freedom— " Now it is religion," said one Hindu, " to-morrow it may be about communism or socialism."[2] According to the Hindu *Indian Social Reformer*, however, tolerance on the part of the state means, " that it recognizes no distinction between faith and faith, and, therefore, cannot allow movements which aim at snatching recruits from other religions to one particular religion ".[3] Upon that argument the unfettered dynamic of Christian evangelism through education would disappear.

It is to be hoped that in the construction of its educational patterns India will value the tolerance and respect for truth which Christian institutions have practised. Liberty to teach is a touchstone of freedom for all India and not for the Christian community alone which is aware of the ever-present danger for Christianity in India to settle placidly into a confined communal existence. Liberty to teach is vital to the virility of Christianity in a land like India, as it is for India's own future as a free people.

One fear of the rising nations in the field of education is the suspected inefficiency of private schools, and there goes with this fear an understandable national pride in showing to the world a well-conducted national system. Turkey and Iran are examples of this. In 1931 Turkey decided that all Turkish children must receive primary education in Turkish schools, and the diplomas of foreign institutions were inadmissible without examination. There was a marked decrease in the number of students attending missionary educational institutions, and a whispering campaign that

[1] *National Christian Council Review*, May 1944, p. 153.
[2] ibid., p. 154.
[3] ibid., p. 155 (quoted).

missionaries were agents of Western imperialism come to exploit the East brought about a drop in the stock of Christian schools. The secularist policy is pursued to the extent of omitting religious teaching altogether in government schools and in forbidding non-Christian children in mission schools to attend Christian prayers or instruction.

But while schools of Christian religious foundation in Turkey are attacked in the press as being centres of foreign culture which denationalize those who attend them, the question is arising whether it is possible to build up a strong national character entirely on a secular basis. One Turkish professor doubts it: " The continuous decline in the sacredness of religion may eventually result in a conclusion of the emptiness of religion and such an outcome may seriously affect the belief in moral concepts also. How can we find a substitute for the religion which was performing these duties so far? What must we do so that a proper attitude of idealism may be prepared in the souls of youth, and keep continuing the sense of responsibility, duty and moral integrity? "[1]

That question is bound to arise in the minds of intelligent men where the secular basis of education is advocated. Does the child belong to the state, or is he a child of God? Can there be a living foundation for human life which does not relate it to the eternal? These companion questions are pertinent for education anywhere, and especially so for education in a secular atmosphere. The Christian answer is clear on the leading question of all which concerns the personality of the child. He is a child of God, and his education must be related to the eternal verities, with definite instruction on the Christian revelation of God. There can be no compromise with the state on these fundamentals of Christian belief and Christian education, and in resisting

[1] Quoted International Review of Missions, October 1935, p. 459.

state pressure the Christian community is serving not only its own belief but the whole cause of freedom.

2

To take some instances of a different character from a " religious " state—Egypt. There the pressure is on Christian schools to exclude Moslem children from attendance at Christian prayers and Bible lessons. In doing this the state believes that it is its prerogative and duty to protect Moslem children from exposure to other than Islamic religious teachings. Conscience clauses—for parents to exercise—are not allowed. It is the state which chooses to limit the liberty to teach on grounds mainly of public order and national solidarity. Some mission schools have been threatened with disciplinary action if they persist in teaching a child any religion other than his own, although there is at present no law to this effect, and parents have raised no objections. When in 1944 the Egyptian government introduced free primary education some foreign schools who entered the scheme were obliged to agree that they would give Christian education only to those Moslem pupils whose parents asked for it in writing. Inspectors were to have the right to question parents making this decision, with the result that at one missionary school in Cairo no Moslem pupils now come to the Scripture lessons.

Commenting on his observations of tendencies in the whole Near East Mr. S. A. Morrison[1] expresses his considered belief that sooner or later, in all Moslem countries in the area, legislation will prohibit the teaching of Christianity to Moslem pupils. Christian schools may even be required to provide instruction in Islam for their Moslem pupils, or to build places of prayer for them within the school premises. It is not inconceivable that for govern-

[1] Church Missionary Society, Cairo, in a manuscript survey.

ment examinations Christian pupils may be required to memorize passages from the Koran.[1]

These internal and external pressures on the part of the state in Egypt are devised chiefly to maintain intact the Islamic edifice of the " church-state ", but the price—from a Western democratic viewpoint—is the absence of a tolerant atmosphere in which liberty to teach is naturally recognized. From the standpoint of the state there are many risks in granting this freedom to-day. One of them is the growing fear of communism, whose agents might use any opening of the national front for further infiltration of communist teaching. Christian teaching, too, is associated with " foreign " and " imperialistic " powers who still dominate the economic life of the Near East. To be free from this dominance and also to be one hundred per cent Islamic in faith, teaching and culture is part of the same nationalistic urge.

Democratic sentiments about individual liberties are freely scattered about the documents and reported conversations I have studied from the Near East. This Western phraseology, however, has no incarnation in the practical liberties which grow out of discussion, debate and free choice, and even that amount of freedom to instruct, which the minorities in Egypt have enjoyed under international

[1] In *Human Rights and Religious Freedom* (p. 7) these important six points are recorded in connection with the right of all citizens to open schools for members of their own religious communities and for others in which:

(i) they may teach their own religion freely, subject to a conscience clause in the case of members of other faiths; (ii) they are free from the obligation to teach any religion, *qua* religion, other than their own; (iii) they may appoint their own staff in all subjects, provided· their scholastic qualifications are adequate; (iv) if the schools are unaided, they may follow their own curricula and their own methods of instruction, provided these do not contravene government requirements regarding health and sanitation, financial administration and technical efficiency; (v) they may participate in government grants to non-government schools without discrimination on religious grounds; (vi) their students are admitted without discrimination to government examinations.

agreement, seems to be in peril of curtailment and possible extinction. In pressing its claim for liberty to teach, Christianity is standing for a universal and not a communal freedom. It is speaking for the rights of every citizen regardless of his religious persuasion, for it is only in a completely tolerant atmosphere that freedom of conscience is respected and true liberty flourishes. This freedom contributes to rather than detracts from a nation's life, for it produces resolute citizens who are not dismayed by the propagation of new and aggressive doctrines because they themselves are rooted and grounded in the Truth which is Eternal.

VI   THE ROMAN CATHOLIC POSITION

A witty Roman Catholic thus summed up the position of his church when faced with the challenge of inconsistency in matters of religious freedom: " When we are in power we behave on our principles; when you are in power we expect you to behave on yours."[1]

Nothing, of course, could be simpler, and the element of truth in the jest has its foundation in the dogmatic position of the Roman church. Principles, of course, mean the authority of the Roman church, unchanging and unyielding in its belief that there is only one source and home of religious truth, which it is the duty of the believer to revere on pain of heresy. Where the Roman church is in power, buttressed by the forces of a Roman Catholic state, then Roman Catholic truth and practice must have their unqualified sway, even to the point of persecution, if necessary, of other religious truth. This, however, must not prevent the Roman church from securing all the benefits of religious toleration in a Protestant country, which is a truthful and practical fulfilment of Augustine's dictum, " When error prevails it is right to invoke liberty of conscience, but when,

[1] Quoted Paton, *The Church and the New Order*, p. 140.

on the contrary, truth predominates, it is proper to use coercion."[1]

While this may be galling to the modern Protestant, who sees the Roman Catholic church developing its life and teaching in his accustomed atmosphere of toleration and at the same time denying similar facilities to Protestants in Roman Catholic lands, its dogmatic undergirding cannot be denied.

If the Roman church regards itself as the only true religion of Christ, then according to its view of religious truth it is rightly intolerant in doctrine, for no one outside the church (other than those involuntarily ignorant) may be saved. Toleration for opposing teaching is rendered unnecessary by the certainty of the church's teaching. Liberty of conscience in religious affairs is not called for and may even be described as impious and absurd. Toleration is logically a method of aiding error, and while it is sometimes necessary to put up with error, and even to live with it within the same state boundaries, the church must not be expected to aid it.

So runs the strict legalism of the Roman position, still unrevoked officially but modified in unofficial expositions and much abated in general practice. Even *The Catholic Encyclopedia*, in its treatment of toleration, contains the paragraph:

Catholics who are conversant with the teachings of their church know how to draw the proper conclusions. Absolutely unflinching in their fidelity to the church as the sole means of salvation on earth, they will treat with respect, as ethically due, the religious convictions of others, and will see in non-Catholics, not enemies of Christ, but brethren. Recognizing from the Catholic doctrine of grace that the possibility of justification and of eternal salvation is not withheld even from heathen,

---

[1] See Macaulay's paraphrase, p. 50.

they will show towards all Christians, e.g. the various Protestant bodies, kindly consideration.[1]

The *Encyclopedia* says further:

> Since the modern state can and must maintain toward the various religions and denominations a more broad-minded attitude than the unyielding character of her doctrine and constitution permits the church to adopt, it must guarantee to individuals and religious bodies not alone interior freedom of belief, but also, as its logical correlative, to manifest that belief outwardly—that is, the right to profess before the world one's religious convictions without the interference of others, and to give visible expression to those convictions in prayer, sacrifice and divine worship.[2]

This sounds liberal enough, but its effectiveness depends on the influence the Roman Catholic hierarchy may have in any given state. Freedom of worship or conscience may be written into a state constitution (as in most Latin-American countries), but the special privileges of the Roman church are rarely modified in order to assist the state to secure full religious freedom for its citizens.

The Roman church views its relationships with the modern state in three ways. It prefers an alliance where the Roman Catholic faith is proclaimed as the religion of the state itself, with all officials professing Roman Catholics, political rights for non-Catholics absent, and all civil laws in harmony with ecclesiastical laws. If this cannot be obtained, then parity is the next best thing which provides equal protection for various religious bodies, even though this opens the door to state interference in the internal affairs of religious organizations. But even that is preferable to the principle of separation between religion and state which, although officially condemned, is nevertheless

---

[1] *The Catholic Encyclopedia*, XIV, pp. 766-7.
[2] ibid., pp. 764-5.

endured because it does give the Church her own constitutional freedom of action.

To understand the modern position of the Roman church
in relation to the state and personal liberty, it must be
realized that it has carried forward the medieval doctrine
of the church-state into its twentieth-century relationships.
The Church is present to strengthen the civil power by its
prayers and teaching, and to claim from the state legal
protection and liberty, financial assistance when needed and
general aid in the establishment of God's Kingdom. It may
also claim from the civil courts an enforcement of its judge-
ments in the ecclesiastical courts. If these services are
forthcoming from the state, then any obedient modern state
is a tolerated partner to the Roman church.

It is part of the genius of the Roman church that it
manages to live and grow in so many widely differing
civilian settings, as varied as the United States of America,
where separation between state and church is complete;
England, where there is an Established church, and, say,
Peru, where a church-state alliance after Rome's own heart
is actively maintained. Part of the secret is due to its sharp
distinction between the legal formulation of Canon Law
defended with agile pertinacity, and what may be called
" planned compromises ", by which the church gets along
in all sorts of societies, adopting the adamant ways of
authority to the contemporary situation without materially
changing the foundations of authority. How subtle and
unchanging Rome is can be seen in this quotation from
Father Ronald Knox's book *The Belief of Catholics*, in
which he discusses the attitude of a strong Catholic majority
to a non-Catholic minority:

> Given such circumstances, is it certain that the Catholic
> government of the nation would have no right to insist
> on Catholic education being universal (which is a form of
> coercion), and even to deport or imprison those who

unsettle the minds of its subjects with new doctrines? It is certain that the church would claim that right for the Catholic government, even if considerations of prudence forbade its exercise in fact. . . . And for these reasons a body of Catholic patriots, entrusted with the government of a Catholic state, will not shrink even from repressive measures in order to perpetuate the secure domination of Catholic principles among their fellow-countrymen.[1]

While neither Roman Catholics nor Protestants have historically a clean sheet in the matter of compulsion in belief, Protestantism has steadily moved away from compulsion as a practical or even desirable policy. Rome remains covertly committed to it, an attitude which colours and directs its policy in those countries where it has any position of dominance, and which is a reserve weapon in countries where it has to walk more circumspectly.

Spain may be taken as an example of the alliance type of relationship between the church and a state. Nominally there is freedom of worship, a matter important to the 30,000 Spanish Protestants in a population of over 27 millions. This was secured in the October 1945 Bill of Rights, which read:

> In accord with article 6 of the Bill of Rights for Spaniards, liberty of worship (*cultos*) is now established (*queda establecida*) for all dissident Churches in the whole of National territory, provided that services are held inside the building with no public manifestation.
> The representatives or ministers of these Churches may exercise their ministry without being molested, provided that they confine themselves to their preaching and pious practices without relating these to political affairs.[2]

But the practical effect of the Bill can be seen in these comments contained in a partially suppressed Associated Press dispatch from Spain, quoted in the Chicago *Christian Century*:

[1] p. 241.   [2] *World Dominion*, July-August 1946, p. 203.

Protestants do not have the right to withdraw their children from Catholic teaching in the public schools, or the right to establish Protestant schools.

They do not have the right to print Protestant literature, even hymnbooks. Publication requires licence by the government censor; the censor will not, and under the law cannot, give his permission without the *Imprimatur* of the Roman Catholic authorities; and they will not grant this for Protestant publications.

Protestants who received Catholic baptism in infancy cannot be legally married except by a priest and, naturally therefore, upon conditions imposed by the church. The theory back of this evidently is that Catholic baptism, even when received by an unconscious infant, imprints an indelible Catholic character which cannot be effaced by subsequent conversion to the Protestant faith. In the eyes of the law, once a Catholic always a Catholic, and no marriage of a Catholic without a priest is legally valid—even if the " Catholic " in question is actually a Protestant.

Protestants do not have equal rights to government jobs, or respect for their faith in the conscript army and public institutions, or the right to hold Protestant ceremonies at burials in civil cemeteries, or assurance of a decent place of burial in towns which lack civil cemeteries.

They do not have the right to carry on missionary work.[1]

As the American paper comments, what is wrong fundamentally with Spain is the lack of civil rights. If they were unchallengeably present, the place of Spanish religious liberties would not be so insecure, or so open to the influence of a dominant church.

1

In Latin America the Evangelical churches have been accustomed for years now to live in an atmosphere where, in differing form, the Roman Catholic church is an estab-

[1] *The Christian Century*, January 22, 1947, pp. 103f.

lished church, drawing an income direct from the state and receiving the state's approval to the appointment of its bishops. Some anti-clerical politicians have looked with approval on the growth of the Evangelical churches, regarding them as an opposition movement to the powerful church. But the Evangelical churches have wisely not, as a body, sought to attack the established position of the Roman Catholic church, but have pleaded in general for the minimum religious rights of a free church in a free state, including freedom to determine faith and creed, freedom of worship, preaching and teaching; freedom from the imposition of religious ceremonies; freedom to instruct youth; freedom of missionary activity, both home and foreign.

In some Latin-American countries the Evangelicals have had the opposition of a dominant church and also the protection of a liberal state regime; in others government and church have combined in opposition, and in some there have been anti-religious groups who wish to eliminate religion altogether. In most instances, the challenge to religious liberty for the Evangelicals has arisen either because of a dominant church's influence or through the state's rebellion against it. Some of the issues have turned on points associated with the state claim to limit the number of ministers employed by any denomination, and to require of them certain standards of education and an insistence on their being native born citizens. In education the state may forbid religious teaching in private schools and require instruction on civics or morals. Another problem of liberty involves the holding of church property which in some Latin-American countries has been nationalized as a result of the inordinate landed wealth of the dominant church standing in the pathway of agrarian reform.

Colombia is a typical example of one of the South American countries where minor disabilities for Protestants are numerous. The Roman Catholic religion is declared to be the religion of the nation and an essential element of public order, but at the same time the church is independent. Liberty of worship is guaranteed, and no one may be molested because of his religious opinions, nor compelled to profess beliefs and observe practices which are against his conscience. Private schools and mission schools are not required to teach the Roman Catholic faith, and while it is difficult (owing to local instigated opposition) for a parent to withdraw a child from religious instruction in a public school, the law permits it.

Public preaching in squares and streets is inadvisable, owing to the traditional attitude of the people to religious ceremonies and the probable disturbance of public order by hooligans often organized by parish priests. But the authorities recognize the right of public preaching. Marriage by a Protestant minister must be preceded by civil marriage, a complicated procedure involving expense, delay and a declaration that the parties never were, or have ceased to be, Roman Catholics. Every Protestant marriage application is referred to the parish priest for investigation, who usually practises his persuasive arts to convince the bride that she is sinning against " la Santa Madre Iglesia ". Roman Catholics suffer no such delays or investigations.

In the public schools Roman Catholic priests as teachers make life unpleasant for Protestant pupils, and Dr. W. S. Rycroft (an authority on religious liberty in Latin America) says:

> In rural communities, when the priest makes one of his infrequent visits, he is zealous in arousing the country people against their Protestant neighbours. Typical of the advice (or orders) he gives to the people is the command on pain of sanction from the church, not to buy goods nor to sell goods to the Protestants, not to employ them nor to work for them. Expressive of the Catholic feeling towards everything Protestant is the charge laid

upon the villagers in a certain place in Bolivar whom the priest visits once a year, that they erect a cross on the plaza, and for the safety of their own souls, utter a curse upon the Protestants every time they pass this wooden symbol. In Bogota scarcely a week goes by without some scathing diatribe, spoken from a Catholic pulpit or by radio, against a Protestant school or church or against the Protestants as individuals.[1]

One of the big issues of religious liberty in Latin America is the question of the entry of foreign missionaries, and this particularly affects Protestant missionary organizations in North America.

In 1942 one of the Brazilian archbishops openly addressed the United States ambassador, suggesting that " the Protestant propaganda, developed by North American missionaries, is a motive which causes antipathy and resentment against the United States of America ".[2] This point of view was exploited by Nazi propagandists who suggested to Roman Catholics that the increased number of Protestant missionaries was part of a move to " Yankeefy " Latin America, and those emissaries were spreading a culture foreign to the Latin American mind. If the United States wished to take a " goodwill " interest in the South, then the programme should be in the hands of Roman Catholics. This subtle appeal to nationalism is one which provides strong ground for Roman Catholicism, intertwined as it is with national tradition and custom, and seemingly part of the state's solidarity. It can only be challenged on the grounds of religious liberty which must include free movement of both home and foreign missionaries.

In summing up the religious liberty position in Latin America, Dr. Rycroft says that in an impartial survey of the various state constitutions an observer might conclude that all was well. But the following points need to be remembered:

[1] Rycroft, in a Manuscript Survey, September 1942.   [2] ibid., p. 13.

In many cases this religious liberty has been won after a long and sometimes bitter struggle between the reactionary forces of the Roman Catholic Church aided by conservative Catholic laymen on the one hand and liberal Latin Americans (nominally Catholic) stimulated and helped by Protestant missionaries and nationals on the other.

The struggle still goes on. The Roman Catholic Church does not lose an opportunity to oppose or persecute Protestants and to hinder their work, in spite of the constitution.

The principle of religious liberty itself is now threatened.[1]

The Roman church is alive to all aspects of the question —religiously, culturally and nationally—and uses every one of them to buttress its own position, and to identify the state with one religion. A similar campaign has been conducted in Italy where Article Five of the new Constitution, while granting legal organization to " other religious confessions ", recognizes the privileged position of the Roman church under the Lateran Pact concluded during the Mussolini regime. These pacts compel all citizens, Roman Catholic and non-Roman-Catholic alike, to pay towards the maintenance of the Roman church, including priests' salaries, and to have their children taught Roman Catholic doctrine in the public schools. In reporting these facts in March 1947 the *Manchester Guardian* Rome correspondent added that one of the least desirable results of the arrangement " will be an increase in anti-clericalism which is already rampant in post-war Italy ".[2]

[1] Rycroft, op. cit.
[2] The Rome correspondent of the *Christian Science Monitor*, on May 3, 1947, reported personal guarantees to Protestants by the Prime Minister, and also the decision of the Assembly to allow private groups to set up schools free from state control and cost. This, in the correspondent's opinion, gives greater facility to the wealthy Roman church, but some observers see in it a tiny step towards eventual separation of church, state and school.

What should be the attitude of other Christians when confronted with the claims of the Roman church and their frequent denial of religious liberty? It is embarrassing and distasteful for separated sections of the Christian Church to appear at loggerheads on such fundamental issues, and both sides need a sharper insight into each other's consciences and beliefs. Protestants especially should remember the bold, uncompromising stand of the Roman church in Central Europe when Nazi domination threatened the independent existence of the Christian Church. In the crucial struggle there may be in the future for the whole Church, Rome's strength and potential resistance may be decisive factors.

On its side, Rome should salute the same qualities in the Protestant churches, and while maintaining its dogmatic position, be gentlemanly enough not to hinder religious liberty in those lands where it is all-powerful. To do as you would be done by is perhaps the only answer to the priestly jest quoted at the beginning of this section.

V

PLAN FOR LIBERTY

IN the Maruitshuis at The Hague hangs Rembrandt's great painting "The School of Anatomy". The last time I saw it I was struck by an immortal touch about Rembrandt's art which had previously escaped me. In the centre of the picture lies the corpse whose arm is being dissected by the master anatomist surrounded by his half-dozen colleagues alert to notice every twist of the master's skill. The concentration, so it seems, is on the dissection of the dead arm—an attitude emphasized by the startled manner in which the spectators look up at someone unseen who has suddenly entered the room. Their faces are lit by the glow of expectant recognition, as if life had removed the dead thing lying in the centre of the picture by a fresh breath of freedom, so that the final impression made on the spectator by Rembrandt's art is not of death (as the subject of the picture might suggest) but of life and liberty.

It has been the implicit argument of this book that religious liberty is the flower of human liberties and that, to use a Christian analogy, it is not the encumbrances of death which burden the human scene, but the presence of life which liberates it. Religious freedom is the fundamental human freedom. This is a claim borne out in history in the testimony of prophets, painters and poets whose individual art has been inspired by the lofty facts of theistic belief. It is a claim to which hosts of ordinary men and women as well add their witness through the dignities and capacities of normal life. Religion touches the springs of life—a reason for the fierce loyalties and bitter antagonisms displayed in its name.

It is claimed by religion that without it life itself has no meaning or purpose, and that it thus sets up a relationship between man and God. The Christian would state his belief more explicitly and affirm that to know, obey and worship God is life, and that without this experience men are still under " the law of death " and have not entered the relationship of " sonship " which God establishes with man through Christ. Even if the Christian affirmations are not used we can recognize that religion is innate in every human being, either in his own solitariness, or in the fellowship of a religious group.

Freedom in religion is, therefore, twofold. First, the right of the individual's direct approach to God, his freedom of conscience and free choice of a community where he shall find religious fellowship. Second, the right of a religious community freely to order its own way of life and to witness to its beliefs. Those are the basic foundations of religious liberty, and it is the argument of this book that " the right to them is an inalienable one at all times and in all circumstances, and ought to be acknowledged and duly safeguarded by the State ".[1]

This right, however, is not an unconditional one.

Civilized man has grouped himself for the ordering of his life into states towards which he has duties and loyalties. His belief in religious freedom must not mean that he is a disturber of the peace, or a danger to public order, or an instigator of actions which may outrage the moral decencies of his fellows. Religion may be a cloak for subversive propaganda and organizations which the state, quite rightly, must curtail and condemn. No honourable citizen will use his religious liberty to undermine the power of the state—unless a high matter of conscience is involved for which he is prepared to act at his own risk.

At this point, however, the state is sometimes professedly apprehensive about religious liberty. The fear that liberty

---

[1] *Human Rights and Religious Freedom*, p. 4.

may be abused, or evidence of its alleged abuse, are enough to justify curtailment of religious freedom. This is particularly the case in lands where one religion is dominant, or where there is a church-state relationship as in some Islamic lands. But this apprehension should not be allowed to develop into an excuse for not granting full religious freedom without the fullest and most exact examination of the circumstances. Liberty is not provided for by hedging it round with restrictions, but by removing them so as to allow full and disciplined development of the human spirit and its communities of association.

Religious liberty is, therefore, a universal human right rather than a privileged claim for minority groups. It is in that way we have to regard it. Any plan for the general liberties and human freedom is not complete without the embodiment of this fundamental freedom which liberates the human spirit at the highest level of its capacities and achievements. To provide room for this liberty to emerge and develop is an undoubted obligation on the modern state.

Under modern conditions there is a tendency to entrust the state with many general responsibilities for human welfare, such as provision for health, education, social services and employment. Unless the state plays its proper part in these fields of public good, men's hopes for freedom from ignorance, disease and want are in vain. Co-operation between the state and its citizens is an essential element in planning for freedom. We may believe that the achievement of these good ends is part of the divine purpose for mankind, but their realization is dependent on human action, on a partnership between individual citizens and the state.

In this sense religious liberty has a right to look to the state for acknowledgements and safeguards. It asks not for a condescending conferment of an additional religious privilege, in the same way as the franchise might be extended or a new school built, but for the elevation of this liberty in all its fullness to the highest categories of liberty for the modern citizen. As an inalienable right religious liberty is a part of every individual's freedom, and to see that he is able to exercise it to the full should be the proud privilege of every modern state.

I

In order to give religious liberty its rightful place amongst the great freedoms of the world in all its fullness, such as this book has advocated, it ought surely to be embodied in any International Bill of Rights which may be framed by an organization such as the United Nations, and made effective by all the signatories in their respective countries. Any general plan for liberty must include religious liberty amongst its first aims, and to place the claims of this freedom on the international level clears a way for action and establishes a new milestone in human freedom.

In particular this suggested action applies to religious minorities. In the survey reference was made to the work done by the League of Nations in solving minority problems through its system of enquiry and report, based on various treaties in which the states concerned bound themselves to respect the liberties of minorities within their borders. Admirable as were the League's intentions and methods, they did frequently offend national pride and prestige. States naturally resented the light of publicity and investigation being thrown on their particular sore spot while their neighbours with equally tender problems got off without much attention. However solemn the treaty, the obligations of public order could easily be invoked to provide a useful alibi for no action. Good intentions on paper were legion, but so often local administrators, and not the statesmen who negotiated the treaties, had the last word. Treaties, too, meant diplomacy, national interests and national policy —a trinity of entanglements sufficient to bog down the claims of any minority.

But this experience of minority problems between the two wars was not all wasted. It was an advance on the unfettered action of the individual state applying only its own mind to its problems and settling them by arbitrary and judicial methods. It demonstrated the truth that human freedoms are the concern of the whole human race, and gave publicity to the fact about minorities, a most valuable contribution to the cause of liberty to which present-day action is indebted.

What is now needed is something different, but yet a development of the previous method.

Briefly " it is the method of making a just treatment for religious minorities incumbent on all states alike, without any particular and possibly invidious reference to particular states ".[1] This would mean, as mentioned already, a declaration by all the United Nations in much more particular terms than vague references to " freedom of worship ", and one which all members of the United Nations would be expected to conform to, and which had the authority of the United Nations behind it, supported, if necessary, by some application of sanctions.

A first draft of such a plan was issued in 1947 by the British Government in a White Paper[2] containing an enumeration of human rights and fundamental freedoms as a preliminary contribution to the discussion of the problem within the United Nations Organization. The paper recognizes that the guarantee of human rights in the internal legal systems of individual states is not enough. There must

---

[1] *Human Rights and Religious Freedom*, p. ii.
[2] *An International Bill of Human Rights*, June 1947 (His Majesty's Stationery Office). This draft is not official policy.

be some guarantee internationally for the "realization of human rights and fundamental freedoms for all without distinction as to race, sex, language or religion ".[1]   In this British draft Bill of Rights, article 13 is on freedom of religion and reads:

(1) Every person shall be free to hold any religious or other belief dictated by his conscience and to change his belief.

(2) Every person shall be free to practise, either alone or in community with other persons of like mind, any form of religious worship and observance, subject only to such restrictions, penalties or liabilities as are strictly necessary to prevent the commission of acts which offend laws passed in the interests of humanity and morals, to preserve public order and to ensure the rights and freedoms of other persons.

(3) Subject only to the same restrictions, every person of full age and sound mind shall be free to give and receive any form of religious teaching and to endeavour to persuade other persons of full age and sound mind of the truth of his beliefs, and in the case of a minor the parent or guardian shall be free to determine what religious teaching he shall receive.[2]

This article includes most of the points on religious liberty pleaded for in this book, and whether or no they are eventually incorporated in a Bill of Rights, they are witness to the views of the British Government.

II

Such a Bill of Rights would be truly international, beginning on that plane and maintaining its thought and action in that atmosphere.   It would avoid the pitfall of making stipulations in treaties binding only on particular states. All states would start on the same level and make the same

---

[1] *U.N. Charter*, Chapter IV, Article 13.
[2] *An International Bill of Human Rights*, p. 10.

affirmations through the United Nations and so add a Magna Carta of religious liberty to the great documents of human freedom. If this were solemnly done, and any breaches of the declaration equally solemnly reported and ventilated, a new way of handling minority and freedom problems might emerge. It is easy, of course, to deride solemn declarations of this kind as not worth very much, and the cynic has plenty of evidence to support his view. But it is worth while recalling that such diverse prophets of liberty as Thomas Jefferson and Lord Acton did not disparage solemn declarations. Jefferson held that the American Declaration had a very definite effect upon American conduct and history, and Lord Acton believed that a single page of the Declaration of Rights of 1789 outweighed libraries and was stronger than all the armies of Napoleon.

The gist of a Charter of Religious Freedom has been given on page 18, and much of its substance, if not its phrasing, would surely appear in a plan of liberty for individual citizens and minorities. But some comments on its claims are called for. Declarations must be tested by their application to individuals and to associations.

Any plan for liberty of religion must, for instance, make it clear that if an individual in choosing his religion or changing it loses the state's protection, or forfeits equality before the law, or is deemed incapable of succeeding to property, then he is a penalized man and has suffered for his belief's sake. No modern state can be deemed loyal to a Declaration of Human Rights which permits those penalties to be suffered.

Again, the right of association for religious purposes will be ineffective if it omits such practical guarantees as the rights of religious communities to be recognized as legal corporations, and to appoint their own leaders and officers without hindrance. Another specific right of a religious community is to maintain freely their connections with co-religionists in other countries and to receive contributions towards their religious, educational, social and charitable activities. A community must also have freedom to erect and maintain buildings for worship and teaching, and to appoint their own staff in them, provided their qualifications conform to the minimum technical requirements of the state.

Liberty not only needs definition in theory, but it needs the most careful definition in practice to secure its full enjoyment. Minorities which suffer small social disabilities because of their religion are as much in bondage as those who have liberty of worship denied them. Their claims must be pressed on the level of citizenship, its freedoms and privileges in a modern state, as well as on the grounds of inherent religious right.

These rights need safeguarding, too, by the state when the right of religious instruction and education is in dispute. Full freedom here should provide that no minor should be taught a religion other than that of his parents or guardians without their consent. There must also be provision for any substantial religious minority to provide special religious teaching for its own children, especially in those countries where religious instruction is given in the state schools. From this follows the freedom for all citizens to open schools for members of their own religious communities, and for others, where they may teach their own religion freely, and to be free, at the same time, from the obligation to teach any religion other than their own. Freedom to appoint staffs and freedom to participate in government grants without discrimination on religious grounds, and to have the right to sit for government examinations without religious discrimination, proceed from the central right of freedom in instruction and education.

III

These are some of the practical, everyday safeguards that religious liberty needs. In countries like Britain or America these details—many of them administrative—are taken for granted as part of the rights of citizenship. No one would dispute them, and any government action which threatened them would be closely scrutinized and criticized in public debate. Over a large part of the earth to-day no such democratic scrutiny would be possible. Therefore a declaration of human rights, however generous in its main clauses, would need explicit safeguards, such as those mentioned above, so that all countries might solemnly, and together, affirm their support of them.

A Declaration of Human Rights within the United Nations containing amongst its cardinal articles the rights of religious freedom should be the aim of all civilized peoples. Much responsibility for its promotion rests with the British and American peoples who have a duty to strengthen the hands of their governments in pressing for the formulation of a Declaration of Human Rights to which all states would be invited to become signatories. To make the declaration comprehensive a recognition of religious freedom, as it has been inadequately expounded in this book, is vitally necessary.

We must beware of phrases that appear satisfactory, and press for their definition in the terms of the Religious Charter as given in Chapter I. Now is the time for action in this matter.

However tired we are of hearing it, there is no doubt that we are at the beginning of a new period in human history. Whatever the new forces may be that he has to face, man's spirit is essentially the same. He is born to be free and to be free above all in religion. Many universal freedoms have been guaranteed to man through international action, and the work of the United Nations Organization is likely to secure more of them. The crown of those guarantees will be a Declaration of Religious Freedom which states will accept as an obligation of their membership of the United Nations.

These are the grounds, too, on which the Christian Church should support any campaign for religious liberty.

It has been freely admitted in this book that the hands of the Christian Church are not clean in the matter of religious liberty. Christian history can easily be ransacked for tales of repression and ecclesiastical tyranny. But to-day the Christian Church is aware of the challenge to religious liberty in many parts of the world, and it approaches the problem, not in any partisan spirit but on the broad basis of the general liberties of mankind.[1] Neither does it wish to claim liberties for itself which are denied to others. It is fighting the battle to-day of all religions and no religion. There must be freedom for belief and unbelief, for those who hold that religion is the crown of human life and for those who see in it only a mass of superstition and ignorance. Only on the grounds of toleration for all religious opinions, and for none, can true religion itself flourish.

[1] Both the U.K. Draft of *An International Bill of Human Rights* and the British Churches' *Statement on Human Rights and Religious Freedom* referred to in this book have been submitted to the U.N. Commission now engaged on preparing the U.N. Declaration.

INDEX

A

ACTON, LORD, 14, 16, 17, 65, 121
Ady, C. M., 49
Afghanistan, 73
Africa, 76f.
Agitator's Guide, 55
Albigensians, 45
Anglicans, 34
Anglican Tradition in the Life of England (Bishop of Durham), 32
Areopagitica (Milton), 34
Atlantic Charter, 51
Augustine, 25, 50
Azad, Mr., 94

B

BAPTISTS, 28, 47, 57
Barker, Sir Ernest, 20, 32, 62
Barmen Synod Declaration, 12
Bates, Searle, 14, 21, 28, 47, 69, 97
Baxter, Richard, 10
Belgian Congo, 75
Belief of Catholics (Knox), 107
Bill of Human Rights, An International, 119f.
Bill of Rights, 43
Bill of Rights (Spain), 108
Brazil, 112
Buddhism, 66
Burma, 83, 86

C

CALVIN, 26ff.
Calvinism, 27, 31, 32
Carlyle, A. J., 45, 46
Catholic Encyclopedia, 105, 106
Charles I, 32
Charles II, 33
Charter of Religious Freedom, 18, 19, 121
Charter of the United Nations, 51, 120
China, 13, 76-8, 83, 97
Christian Century, 108
Christian Church and Liberty (Carlyle), 46
Christian Counter-Attack, 43
Christian Science Monitor, 113
Church and the New Order (Paton), 104
Church, Community and State (Oldham), 63
Church Missionary Society, 81, 102
Church of England, 9
Church of Scotland General Assembly, 9, 31
Church Parades, Compulsory, 23, 24
Church, State and Study (Barker), 20
Churches in the Modern State (Figgis), 32
Clarendon Code, 35
Colombia, 110

125